AMAZING ANIMALS OF THE WORLD ①

Volume 4

Fisher — Hummingbird, Ruby-Throated

GROLIER

an imprint of

■SCHOLASTIC

Scholastic Library Publishing

www.scholastic.com/librarypublishing

First published 2008 by Grolier, an imprint of Scholastic Inc.

For information address the publisher: Grolier, Scholastic Library Publishing
90 Old Sherman Turnpike
Danbury, CT 06816

Printed and bound in the U.S.A.

Library of Congress Cataloging-in-Publication Data
Amazing animals of the world 1.
v. cm.
Contents: v. 1. Aardvark-bobcat — v. 2. Bobolink-cottonmouth — v. 3. Coyote-fish, Siamese fighting — v. 4. Fisher-hummingbird, ruby-throated — v. 5. Hyena, brown-mantis, praying — v. 6. Marmoset, common-owl, great horned — v. 7. Owl, pygmy-robin, American — v. 8. Sailfin, giant-spider, black widow — v. 9. Spider, garden-turtle, common musk — v. 10. Turtle, green sea-zebrafish.
Includes bibliographical references and index.
ISBN 0-7172-6225-1; 978-0-7172-6225-0 (set : alk. Paper) - ISBN 0-7172-6226-X; 978-0-7172-6226-7 (v. 1 : alk. paper) - ISBN 0-7172-6227-8; 978-0-7172-6227-4 (v. 2 : alk. paper) - ISBN 0-7172-6228-6; 978-0-7172-6228-1 (v. 3 : alk. paper) - ISBN 0-7172-6229-4; 978-7172-6229-8 (v. 4 : alk. paper) - ISBN 0-7172-6230-8; 978-7172-6230-4 (v. 5 : alk. paper) - ISBN 0-7172-6231-6; 978-0-7172-6231-1 (v. 6 : alk. paper) - ISBN 0-7172-6232-4; 978-0-7172-6232-8 (v. 7 : alk. paper) - ISBN 0-7172-6233-2; 978-0-7172-6233-5 (v. 8 : alk. paper) - ISBN 0-7172-6234-0; 978-0-7172-6234-2 (v. 9 : alk. paper) - ISBN 0-7172-6235-9; 978-0-7172-6235-9 (v. 10 : alk. paper)
1. Animals—Encyclopedias, Juvenile. I. Grolier Incorporated. II. Title: Amazing animals of the world one.
QL49.A453 2007
590.3—dc22

2007012982

About This Set

Amazing Animals of the World 1 brings you pictures of 400 exciting creatures, and important information about how and where they live.

Each page shows just one species, or individual type, of animal. They all fall into seven main categories, or groups, of animals (classes and phylums scientifically) identified on each page with an icon (picture)—amphibians, arthropods, birds, fish, mammals, other invertebrates, and reptiles. Short explanations of what these group names mean, and other terms used commonly in the set, appear in the Glossary.

Scientists use all kinds of groupings to help them sort out the thousands of types of animals that exist today and once wandered the earth (extinct species). *Kingdoms, classes, phylums, genus,* and *species* are among the key words here that are also explained in the Glossary.

Where animals live is important to know as well. Each of the species in this set lives in a particular place in the world, which you can see outlined on the map on each page. And in those places, the animals tend to favor a particular habitat—an environment the animal finds suitable for life—with food, shelter, and safety from predators that might eat it. There they also find ways to coexist with other animals in the area that might eat somewhat different food, use different homes, and so on.

Each of the main habitats is named on the page and given an icon, or picture, to help you envision it. The habitat names are further defined in the Glossary.

As well as being part of groups like species, animals fall into other categories that help us understand their lives or behavior. You will find these categories in the Glossary, where you will learn about carnivores, herbivores, and other types of animals.

And there is more information you might want about an animal—its size, diet, where it lives, and how it carries on its species—the way it creates its young. All these facts and more appear in the data boxes at the top of each page.

Finally, the set is arranged alphabetically by the most common name of the species. That puts most beetles, for example, together in a group so you can compare them easily.

But some animals' names are not so common, and they don't appear near others like them. For instance, the chamois is a kind of goat or antelope. To find animals that are similar—or to locate any species—look in the Index at the end of each book in the set. It lists all animals by their various names (you will find the Giant South American River Turtle under Turtle, Giant South American River, and also under its other name—Arrau). And you will find all birds, fish, and so on gathered under their broader groupings.

Similarly, smaller like groups appear in the Set Index as well—butterflies include swallowtails and blues, for example.

Table of Contents
Volume 4

Glossary..4

Fisher..5

Flamingo, Greater..6

Fly, Common Fruit...7

Fly, Tsetse...8

Fox, Arctic...9

Fox, Gray...10

Fox, Kit..11

Fox, Red...12

Frog, Cuban Tree..13

Frog, Green..14

Frog, Poison Dart...15

Frog, Wood...16

Gar, Florida..17

Gazelle, Thomson's...18

Gecko, Moorish Wall...19

Gerbil...20

Gibbon, Hoolock...21

Giraffe..22

Gnu, Brindled...23

Goldfish..24

Goose, Canada..25

Goose, Snow...26

Gorilla..27

Grosbeak, Evening..28

Grosbeak, Rose-breasted...29

Guinea Pig..30

Gull, Laughing..31

Guppy...32

Hamster, Common..33

Hare, Snowshoe..34

Heron, Great Blue...35

Heron, Green-Backed..36

Herring, Atlantic..37

Hippopotamus..38

Hippopotamus, Pygmy..39

Hornbill, Great...40

Hornbill, Rhinoceros...41

Horsefly, American..42

Hummingbird, Broad-tailed...43

Hummingbird, Ruby-throated..44

Set Index..45

Glossary

Amphibians—species usually born from eggs in water or wet places, which change (metamorphose) into land animals. Frogs and salamanders are typical. They breathe through their skin mainly and have no scales.

Arctic and Antarctic—icy, cold, dry areas at the ends of the globe that lack trees but are home to small plants that grow in thawed areas (tundra). Penguins and seals are common inhabitants.

Arthropods—animals with segmented bodies, hard outer skin, and jointed legs, such as spiders and crabs.

Birds—born from eggs, these creatures have wings and often can fly. Eagles, pigeons, and penguins are all birds, though penguins cannot fly through the air.

Carnivores—they are animals that eat other animals. Many species do eat each other sometimes, and a few eat dead animals. Lions kill their prey and eat it, while vultures clean up dead bodies of animals.

Cities, Towns, and Farms—places where people live and have built or used the land and share it with many species. Sometimes these animals live in human homes or just nearby.

Class—part, or division, of a phylum.

Deserts—dry, usually warm areas where animals often are more active on cooler nights or near water sources. Owls, scorpions, and jack rabbits are common in American deserts.

Endangered—some animals in this set are marked as endangered because it is possible they will become extinct soon.

Extinct—these species have died out completely for whatever reason.

Family—part of an order.

Fish—water animals (aquatic) that typically are born from eggs and breathe through gills. Trout and eels are fish, though whales and dolphins are not (they are mammals).

Forests and Mountains—places where evergreen (coniferous) and leaf-shedding (deciduous) trees are common, or that rise in elevation to make cool, separate habitats. Rain forests are different (see below).

Freshwater—lakes, rivers, and the like carry fresh water (unlike Oceans and Shores, where the water is salty). Fish and birds abound, as do insects, frogs, and mammals.

Genus—part of a family.

Grasslands—habitats with few trees and light rainfall. Grasslands often lie between forests and deserts, and they are home to birds, coyotes, antelope, and snakes, as well as many other kinds of animals.

Herbivores—these animals eat mainly plants. Typical are hoofed animals (ungulates) that are common on grasslands, such as antelope or deer. Domestic (nonwild) ones are cows and horses.

Hibernators—species that live in harsh areas with very cold winters slow down their functions then become inactive or dormant.

Invertebrates—animals that lack backbones or internal skeletons. Many, such as insects and shrimp, have hard outer coverings. Clams and worms are also invertebrates.

Kingdom—the largest division of species. All living things are classified in one of the five kingdoms: animals, plants, fungi, protists, and monerans.

Mammals—these creatures usually bear live young and feed them on milk from the mother. A few lay eggs (monotremes like the platypus) or nurse young in a pouch (marsupials like opossums and kangaroos).

Migrators—some species spend different seasons in different places, moving to where more food, warmth, or safety can be found. Birds often do this, sometimes over long distances, but other types of animals also move seasonally, including fish and mammals.

Oceans and Shores—seawater is salty, often deep, and huge. In it live many fish, invertebrates, and some mammals, such as whales and dolphins. On the shore, birds and other creatures often gather.

Order—part of a class.

Phylum—part of a kingdom.

Rain forests—here huge trees grow among many other plants helped by the warm, wet environment. Thousands of species of animals also live in these rich habitats.

Reptiles—these species have scales, have lungs to breathe, and lay eggs or give birth to live young. Dinosaurs are thought to have been reptiles, while today the class includes turtles, snakes, lizards, and crocodiles.

Scientific Name—the genus and species name of a creature in Latin. For instance, *Canis lupus* is the wolf. Scientific names avoid the confusion possible with common names in any one language or across languages.

Species—a group of the same type of living thing. Part of an order.

Subspecies—a variety but quite similar part of a species.

Territorial—many animals mark out and defend a patch of ground as their home area. Birds and mammals may call very small or very large spots their territories.

Vertebrates—animals with backbones and skeletons under their skins.

Fisher
Martes pennanti

Length of the Body: 3 feet
Length of the Tail: 1 foot
Weight: 1½ to 3¾ pounds
Number of Young: 1 to 6
Diet: rodents, birds, eggs, fish, insects, and fruits

Home: Canada and northern United States
Order: carnivores
Family: badgers, otters, skunks, weasels, and relatives

 Forests and Mountains

 Mammals

© D. ROBERT & LORRI FRANZ / CORBIS

Despite its name, the fisher, a type of marten, prefers to eat porcupines rather than fish. The fisher is one of the few predators clever and vicious enough to kill these spine-covered animals. A fisher will chase a porcupine up a tree and then attack it from above. The fisher bites at the porcupine's face, one of the few parts of its body not protected by sharp quills. In this way the fisher inflicts so many small wounds that the unfortunate porcupine eventually dies. The fisher then gobbles its meal with gusto, leaving nothing more than a bloody shell of skin and spines.

Fisher marten are particularly well adapted for hunting in the trees. A fisher can turn its paws 180 degrees so that they face backward. It then digs its long, sharp claws into the bark of a tree trunk, for an amazingly firm grip. From this anchor the fisher can literally hang upside down to attack porcupines, birds, and other prey. Nature has also designed the fisher's paws to work well on snow. The broad paws enable this creature to run across a fresh blanket of deep snow without sinking.

The fisher is the largest of the true marten. Like their cousins the weasels, marten are hunted for their beautiful fur. Marten have much larger, bushier tails than weasels. They also tend to be bigger, faster, and more agile than their weaselly relatives.

Greater Flamingo
Phoenicopterus ruber

Height: to 5¼ feet
Weight: 5 to 9 pounds
Diet: algae, protists, and small invertebrates
Number of Eggs: 1
Home: Mediterranean region, Middle East, India, parts of Africa and Madagascar, and Caribbean region
Order: auks, herons, and relatives
Family: flamingos

Freshwater

Birds

© WOLFGANG KAEHLER / CORBIS

A group of flamingos in flight looks like a cloud. It is often colored pale pink or bright red. In the lagoons of the Yucatán Peninsula of Mexico, flamingos are nearly red. In Europe they are almost white. Their color depends on the foods they eat.

Flamingos nest in colonies of thousands of birds. These are usually found in swampy areas. Flamingos are good waders. They have the longest neck and legs in proportion to their body of any bird. Their nest is established shortly before eggs are laid. It is a 15-inch-high cone of mud, stones, and shells. A single offspring is produced. It is nourished by food regurgitated by its parents. When the offspring get older, they leave the nest. Then young flamingos assemble in large groups.

Flamingos are "filter feeders." They have a curved beak with screens on the edges. The screens filter solids from swamp water. These solids may include tiny invertebrates, such as crustaceans and mollusks. How does a flamingo obtain food? It moves its bill upside down through the water. Only suitably sized food passes through the screens. The flamingo has a large tongue. It uses it to pump out the sand and mud.

Flamingos have had multiple uses. Ancient Romans used to eat the flamingo's tongue. It was considered a luxury food. Flamingo feathers have been used for decoration. Parks and racetracks have been graced with flamingos. They are encouraged to nest there. They add color and beauty to these sites.

Common Fruit Fly
Drosophila melanogaster

Length: less than 1/10 inch
Diet: rotting fruit
Method of Reproduction: egg layer
Home: worldwide

Order: gnats, mosquitoes, true flies
Family: pomace flies, small fruit flies, vinegar flies

 Cities, Towns, and Farms

 Arthropods

© DONALD SPECKER / ANIMALS ANIMALS / EARTH SCENES

Have you ever seen a tiny fly hovering over a ripe piece of fruit? This creature is called a fruit fly. It is attracted by the smell of the fruit. Just like you, it is eager to eat the juicy food. Fruit flies also eat decaying vegetables and other plants. Ripe fruit doesn't last very long—either in your home or in nature. Fruit flies have adapted to this fact by having a very short life cycle. After mating, the female fruit fly lays 200 or more eggs in fruit. In two days the eggs hatch into tiny, wormlike larvae called grubs. The grubs change, or metamorphose, into adult flies in four to five days. Two days later the adults are ready to mate. They live for only about two weeks.

Fruit flies may be unwelcome visitors in your home. But they are extremely important organisms for geneticists. Geneticists are scientists who study how inherited characteristics are passed from one generation to the next. Fruit flies make good laboratory animals because they produce many eggs. They also have a short life cycle and are easy to raise. But there is another important reason. The fruit fly's salivary glands contain chromosomes that are about 100 times the normal length. Chromosomes are structures within the cell nucleus that carry the genes (units of inheritance). Fruit-fly chromosomes and genes are very large. They are therefore easy to see and study.

Tsetse Fly
Glossina morsitans

Length: ¼ to ½ inch
Diet: blood
Method of Reproduction: live-bearer
Home: Africa

Order: gnats, mosquitoes, true flies
Family: face flies, horn flies, tsetse flies, and relatives

 Grasslands

Arthropods

© ROBERT PATRICK / SYGMA / CORBIS

The tsetse fly is a relative of the housefly. Unlike its harmless cousin, however, the tsetse is a deadly insect. Tsetse flies must drink the blood of animals or humans once every four days. But it is not their bite that inflicts harm, at least not directly. Tsetse flies are feared because they carry a tiny single-celled animal called a trypanosome. This causes disease in both animals and humans. The tsetse picks up trypanosomes from an infected animal or person when it drinks its blood. The trypanosomes do not harm the fly. But when the tsetse takes its next blood meal, the trypanosome can enter the new victim.

One kind of trypanosome causes sleeping sickness in people. Another causes a deadly disease in cows. It is now impossible to raise cattle in many parts of Africa where the tsetse fly is common. Given a choice, however, the tsetse fly will ignore both humans and cattle. It would rather have its favorite food—the blood of warthogs.

The larvae of tsetse flies—young flies that have not yet grown legs or wings—ride around on their mothers' bodies. They feed on food she secretes from special glands. Soon they are ready to transform, or metamorphose, into adults. At this time they drop onto the ground. They dig themselves into the dirt and begin their transformation. They grow wings and legs. When they emerge, they are ready to bite.

Arctic Fox
Vulpes lagopus

Length: 20 to 28 inches
Length of the Tail: 11 to 16 inches
Weight: 6 to 18 pounds
Diet: mainly lemmings
Number of Young: 4 to 8

Home: Arctic regions of North America, Europe, and Asia
Order: carnivores
Family: coyotes, dogs, foxes, jackals, and wolves

  Arctic and Antarctic

Mammals

© MARY ANN MCDONALD / CORBIS

Arctic foxes are the only members of the dog family that change color. They do this twice a year—once for summer and once for winter. There are two subspecies of Arctic foxes: white foxes and blue foxes. In summer, they look alike, with coats of gray brown fur. But in winter the white fox has a white coat. The blue fox has a light gray or brown coat with a bluish tinge. White foxes typically spend the winter in snowy places. Their white coat blends into the snow. Blue foxes usually spend the winter near seacoasts. The weather is milder there.

The Arctic fox has another important adaptation to help it survive in the far north. The animal's very small ears are heavily covered with fur. Small ears lose much less body heat than large ears do. Arctic foxes live in caves or burrows that they make in the side of a hill or cliff. During a blizzard, they often burrow into the snow for protection.

Arctic foxes feed mainly on small rodents called lemmings. They also eat birds, bird eggs, insects, and berries. Sometimes their usual prey is in short supply. These creatures will then follow polar bears and eat the remnants of their prey. But the foxes must not get too close to the bears. Polar bears eat Arctic foxes if they can catch them. The main enemies of Arctic foxes are humans. People kill the foxes for their thick and lustrous fur.

Gray Fox
Urocyon cinereoargenteus

Length of the Body: 1½ to 2¼ feet
Length of the Tail: 1 to 1½ feet
Weight: 5 to 15 pounds
Diet: small vertebrates, insects, and plants

Number of Young: 1 to 10
Home: southern Canada to Venezuela
Order: carnivores
Family: coyotes, dogs, foxes, jackals, and wolves

 Forests and Mountains

 Mammals

© JOE MCDONALD / CORBIS

The gray fox is also known as the tree fox because it has a habit—quite unusual among foxes—of climbing trees. Sometimes the gray fox will scamper up a tree for good reason, such as when it is being chased by a predator. But this fox doesn't need an excuse to go climbing. It can be seen jumping from branch to branch just for the fun of it.

Tree climbing is not the only thing that distinguishes this species from other foxes. The gray fox is more of a vegetarian than its cousins. Most foxes will eat some vegetables with their meat if they are very hungry. But the gray fox often exists solely on fruits, grains, and berries. Not that it will turn up its nose at meat—the gray fox is notorious for eating anything it finds, including scorpions, centipedes, and garbage such as leather, newspaper, and tinfoil.

The gray fox prefers to hunt, eat, and play during the evening and night. Most of these creatures keep a number of hiding places where they can rest during the day. A gray fox's main den may be found deep inside thick grass or a bush, in a pile of rocks, or in a burrow. In keeping with its tree-climbing reputation, the gray fox may even make its home in an old bird's nest! Some gray-fox dens have been found in tree hollows more than 30 feet off the ground.

Kit Fox
Vulpes macrotis

Length of the Body: about 16 inches
Length of the Tail: about 10 inches
Height: about 10 inches
Weight: 4 to 5 pounds
Diet: small mammals, insects, and berries

Number of Young: 4 to 7
Home: southwestern United States and Mexico
Order: carnivores
Family: coyotes, dogs, foxes, jackals, and wolves

 Grasslands

 Mammals

© JONATHAN BLAIR / CORBIS

The kit fox lives in the dry chaparral and brushy hills of Mexico and the American Southwest. The name *kit* comes from the word kitten. It is a play on the fox's tiny size. Although small, the kit fox is incredibly fast. When fleeing danger, it can reach speeds of more than 25 miles per hour.

The kit fox population is declining. In fact, this fox has already disappeared from many areas. One subspecies, the San Joaquin kit fox of central California, is now in danger of extinction and is officially protected. The gravest threat to the fox's survival is the spread of cities into its range.

The kit fox is closely related to the swift fox, which lives on the American short-grass prairie. The kit fox is smaller and faster than its prairie cousin. And it has somewhat lighter-colored fur. Some experts consider kits and swifts to be two members of the same species. However, these two types of foxes do not generally interbreed.

The shy kit fox is a nocturnal animal. This means that it is most active at night. The fox uses its large ears and probing eyes to hunt in the dark of night. But come morning, the creature retires to its burrow, which is usually dug in sandy soil. Its small underground den is built with three or four entrances and escape tunnels. Kit foxes generally mate for life. Their pups are born in March or April.

Red Fox
Vulpes vulpes

Length: 18 to 36 inches
Weight: 9 to 11½ pounds
Diet: carnivorous
Number of Young: 4 to 8
Home: Eurasia, North Africa, North America, Central America, and Australia

Order: carnivores
Family: coyotes, dogs, foxes, jackals, and wolves

 Forests and Mountains

 Mammals

© UWE WALZ / CORBIS

The red fox lives in many places. These include Eurasia, North Africa, North America, and Central America. They can even be found in Australia. It has adapted to all habitats. These range from dense forests to tundra. They are also found in altitudes of up to 15,000 feet.

An adult male fox establishes a territory. There he will live with his family. It is usually one or two females, or vixens, and their offspring. The family lives in a main burrow. There the female gives birth and raises her young. A clever fox digs several emergency holes. These are used for shelter in case of danger. These tunnels can be as long as 30 feet. They all lead to the living chamber.

Mating takes place in the winter. In the spring, the female gives birth. A litter can contain four to eight pups. After about ten days, the pups open their eyes. They are weaned at two months of age. The family stays together until the autumn. Then the young leave to establish a new territory. That is where they will spend their lives.

Foxes can consume a pound or two of rodents and rabbits each day. This helps to control the population of these animals. They also eat berries, earthworms, and insects. Fish and carrion (dead animals) are also part of their diet. Foxes have a reputation for attacking fowl and game. Pheasants are a favored target. The red fox is the preferred prey in the sport of fox hunting. Foxes also are trapped for their valuable fur. But the fox is clever and intelligent. Its hearing, sight, and sense of smell are highly developed. It knows how to escape hunters, dogs, and traps.

Cuban Tree Frog
Osteopilus septentrionalis

Length: 2 to 5 inches (female); 1½ to 3½ inches (male)
Diet: insects
Method of Reproduction: egg layer

Home: Cuba and the Bahamas; introduced into Florida and elsewhere
Order: frogs and toads
Family: New World tree frogs

  Cities, Towns, and Farms

Amphibians

© JOE MCDONALD / CORBIS

The Cuban tree frog's native home is Cuba and the Bahamas. But this species is the largest tree frog in the United States. It probably arrived in the United States as a stowaway aboard boats, hidden in shipments of bananas and other fruits. Its preferred home is forests and plantations where rain is plentiful. But the Cuban tree frog frequently lives near people—in drainpipes, water tanks, and cellars. It may even make a potted plant on a porch its home, especially if the plant is watered daily.

The Cuban tree frog has unusual feet. Each toe ends in a large, sticky disk. The disks help the frog cling tightly to tree bark. The frog has enormous, bulging eyes that help it spot insects. And its long, powerful back legs help it catch prey. A tree frog can jump from one branch to another, catching an insect along the way.

At mating time, male Cuban tree frogs move to ponds or other fresh water. There they begin calling to attract females. The males have loud, harsh voices. Some people say their calls sound like noisy snoring. Each male has a special sac in his throat. He inhales, then forces the air from the lungs over the vocal cords and into the sac. The sac inflates, forming two little balloons on the sides of the throat. The male repeats the process again and again. Each time that air moves over the vocal cords, sound is produced. When a female reaches the male, mating takes place. The female lays her eggs in the water, and the male immediately fertilizes them.

Green Frog
Rana clamitans

Length: 2½ to 4 inches
Diet: insects
Method of Reproduction: egg layer
Home: eastern United States and the Maritime Provinces of Canada

Order: frogs and toads
Family: true frogs

  Freshwater

Amphibians

© JOE MCDONALD / CORBISS

The green frog is a familiar animal to many North Americans. It lives in colonies along the shores of small, shallow ponds and streams. All frogs and toads undergo a remarkable change of appearance as they grow. This process is called metamorphosis.

Green frogs lay their eggs (spawn) in spring or summer. They call mates by making a loud noise, or croak. It sounds like a loose banjo string. Green frogs spawn in fresh water. The eggs are not guarded. Instead, they are surrounded with a jellylike material. The eggs hatch after a few days. The larvae, or tadpoles, emerge. Much like fish, the tadpoles breathe through gills. At first the gills are on the outside of the body. They soon become covered with a fold of

skin. Eventually the lungs grow and the mouth widens. Legs develop and the tail begins to disappear. So when is the frog ready for life on land? When the tail is completely gone. As an adult, the frog will spawn. Then it will return to that same body of water to lay its eggs.

Male green frogs have a specific territory. They defend it by standing together on their hind legs and hugging one another. Green frogs are equipped with a long, sticky tongue. It is attached to the front of the mouth. Frogs use it to catch prey. How do they do it? The frog waits for an insect to fly by. Then the frog simply flicks out its tongue and makes the kill. The green frog catches and eats a large number of insects.

Poison Dart Frog
Phyllobates terribilis

Length: up to 14 inches
Diet: ants and other small arthropods
Method of Reproduction: egg layer

Home: Colombia, South America
Order: frogs and toads
Family: poison dart frogs

 Rain Forests

Amphibians

In the rain forest of South and Central America, there are more than 50 kinds of frogs whose skin secretes a deadly poison. The deadliest poison of all comes from the frog known as *Phyllobates terribilis*. And it is terrible. The poison from just one of these frogs can kill many people. Just touching it causes a nasty irritation.

The Choco Indians of western Colombia, in northwestern South America, put the poison on their blowpipe darts. Long ago, they probably used these poison darts to fight their enemies. Today they use them to hunt animals and birds.

Phyllobates terribilis is the largest of the poison dart frogs, growing to more than a foot in length. Like the others, it is very brightly colored—usually a vivid red or golden yellow. These colors seem to be a warning to other animals not to come too close. And only one animal dares to. A frog-eating snake that does not seem to be bothered by the frog's deadly poison.

Frogs usually lay their eggs in water. When they hatch, tadpoles emerge. The tadpoles live in the water until they metamorphose, or change, into frogs. Poison dart frogs do things differently. They lay their eggs on the ground. When the tadpoles emerge from the hatched eggs, they wriggle onto their parents' backs for a quick trip to the water.

Wood Frog
Rana sylvati

Length: up to 3 inches
Diet: insects and other small animals
Number of Eggs: 2,000 to 3,000

Home: Canada, Alaska, and northeastern United States
Order: frogs and toads
Family: true frogs

 Forests and Mountains

 Amphibians

© LYNDA RICHARDSON / CORBIS

The wood frog looks as though it's wearing a robber's mask. A black or dark brown patch of color extends backward from the snout to the shoulder. This feature makes the wood frog easy to recognize—if you can spot it at all. Usually, this small frog lives in or near moist, wooded areas. Its coloring blends well with the leaves and pine needles on the ground, making the frog almost invisible. The wood frog has extremely long back legs. Disturb a wood frog, and you will be surprised at how far it can jump!

The range of the wood frog extends farther north than that of any other North American frog. The frog is found in Alaska and much of Canada, as well as farther south in the United States. In winter, it may hibernate under stones, rotting logs, or dead leaves. In spring, as the sun begins to warm the land, the wood frog emerges from its winter home and heads for nearby ponds to breed. The male attracts females by croaking. This is the only time of the year when the frogs croak, a sound somewhat like the quack of a duck.

Each female lays tiny black-and-white eggs in the water, which her mate immediately fertilizes. Each egg is surrounded by two coats of jelly, which helps protect the egg. After the eggs are laid, the frogs leave the ponds. In about a week, tadpoles hatch from the eggs.

Florida Gar
Lepisosteus platyrhincus

Length: up to 3 feet
Diet: small fish, insects, and crustaceans
Method of Reproduction: egg layer

Home: Florida and southeastern Georgia
Order: gars
Family: gar pikes, garfishes

 Freshwater

Fish

© E.R. DEGGINGER / PHOTO RESEARCHERS

Other fish are disappearing from populated areas. But the Florida gar may be growing more abundant. This cigar-shaped fish can be seen by the thousands in human-made canals and ditches. It often floats on the surface, motionless, soaking in the warmth of the sun. What is the reason for the gar's success? It can come to the surface of the water and gulp air through its mouth. This enables the fish to survive in water whose quality is poor.

The Florida gar looks lazy as it basks in the sun. But it can move quickly. Its hunting technique is one of ambush. First it hides in the mud or among underwater weeds. From there it will snag a passing fish with a rapid twist of its body and a sideways grab. The Florida gar also feeds on crustaceans such as crayfish and blue crabs. In April and May, a female Florida gar swims into shallow water. She's usually followed by several males as she scatters thousands of eggs across the sandy bottom. She leaves the eggs to be fertilized by the males behind her. Some Florida gars continue to spawn throughout the summer and early fall. The result can be a population explosion that ends only after food runs out.

Gars are known for their tough, diamond-shaped scales. Once, Indians used the scales of large gars as arrowheads. Some early farmers even used gar skins as a protective cover for their wooden plows.

Thomson's Gazelle
Gazella thomsoni

Length: 35 to 42 inches
Height: 23 to 28 inches
Weight: up to 65 pounds
Diet: grasses
Number of Young: 1
Home: Tanzania and Kenya

Order: even-toed hoofed mammals
Family: antelope, bison, buffalo, cattle, goats, and sheep

 Grasslands

 Mammals

© CARL & ANN PURCELL / CORBIS

At dawn or at dusk, herds of Thomson's gazelles move gracefully in Africa's savannas. They are easily identified by their small size and the large black stripe along the lower part of their body. Very playful, young gazelles race and jump very high. Sometimes others in the herd think that this jumping and racing is an alarm signal. The panicked gazelles then run off at top speed.

Thomson's gazelles are nervous and watchful. The smallest strange movement in the herd sends all the gazelles running. Even if only one member of the group starts to run around, flicking its tail, the rest flee. They can run faster than 35 miles per hour and can outrun both lions and leopards. But the small gazelle cannot easily escape from the speedy cheetah. The gazelle tries to dodge the chasing cat by making sudden turns. But the cheetah usually wins because it can run faster than 40 miles per hour.

Thomson's gazelles graze on cut grass left behind by zebras and gnus. When the dry season comes, they also eat small fruits and seeds. During the mating season, males mark a territory and mate with all the females that cross into it. Sometimes there are fights between males, but the fights are usually not too serious. Females can have two pregnancies each year. Females and their young assemble in herds of about 65, while young males form separate groups of about 500 animals.

Moorish Wall Gecko
Tarentola mauritanica

Length: 4 to 6¼ inches
Diet: insects
Number of Eggs: 2 to 3
Home: southern Europe and North Africa

Order: scaled reptiles
Family: geckos

Forests and Mountains

Reptiles

© BARTOMEU BORRELL / BIOS / PETER ARNOLD, INC.

The Moorish wall gecko can be found scrambling about the ancient ruins of Greece. It also runs in the famous olive groves of Spain and the coastal pine woods of Italy. This lizard often ventures into Mediterranean towns and villages. It even moves into dry and deserted buildings. Wherever it is found, the Moorish wall gecko usually clings to a vertical surface such as a wall or a tree trunk. Its toes are shaped like little spatulas. They are covered with tiny suction disks. These disks allow the animal to walk up a wall or even across a ceiling or under a branch.

The gecko is well liked because it eats lots of insects. It is somewhat shy of humans. But it is attracted to houselights where insects have gathered. During the summer the Moorish wall gecko is active only in the cool of night. But in the winter months, it hunts in broad daylight. The gecko, in turn, is hunted by many large birds and snakes. Luckily, its mottled grayish skin is a good camouflage. The animal blends well with both tree trunks and rocks.

Moorish wall geckos mate in spring. Males have violent fights at this time. The female lays her eggs behind a flap of loose tree bark or inside a dried-out wall. Most lizards hatch from soft, moist eggs. But gecko eggs are hard. This keeps the eggs from drying out in their arid habitat.

Gerbil
Gerbillus gerbillus

Length: 2½ to 3 inches
Length of the Tail: 3 to 3½ inches
Weight: 4 ounces
Diet: seeds

Number of Young: 4 or 5
Home: Africa and Asia
Order: rodents
Family: mice, rats

 Deserts

 Mammals

© ROBERT MAIER / ANIMALS ANIMALS / EARTH SCENES

What image pops into your mind when you think of a gerbil? You probably see a cute furry pet. Maybe you imagine it scampering on a wheel in a wire cage. That creature is the Mongolian gerbil. It is just one of 81 species. Another species is *Gerbillus gerbillus*. It is one of the smallest gerbils, and its size helps it survive. Its size allows it to live on the small amount of food available in the desert.

Gerbils live in burrow homes. Each night they go out to gather seeds. Why do they gather the seeds at night? At night the seeds are moist with dew. The seeds and their dew are the gerbils' only source of water.

The gerbil loves its privacy. It marks its home with a scented spray. It squirts it from a gland on its belly. This warns unwelcome visitors to keep away. And what happens if another gerbil trespasses? The two will fight until one backs down. The loser is sprayed with the winner's scent. This serves as a warning to others.

But the gerbil has more dangerous foes to worry about. Larger predators think the gerbil is a tasty meal. So how does the gerbil protect itself? Nature gave it a reddish brown coat. This allows it to blend in with the desert sand. It also helps conceal it from such enemies as the hawk. So how does the hawk spot a gerbil? It is usually attracted by its tail. It is darker than the rest of the gerbil's body. This sometimes lets the rest of a lucky gerbil escape. The hawk is left with only a bit of tail in its talons.

Hoolock Gibbon
Hylobates hoolock

Length: 1½ to 2 feet
Weight: 13 to 15 pounds
Diet: fruits, leaves, flowers, and insects
Number of Young: 1

Home: India, Myanmar (Burma), and Bangladesh
Order: primates
Family: gibbons, lesser apes

Rain Forests

Mammals

© EPA / CORBIS

Endangered Animals

The hoolock gibbon is a slender animal with long arms. If it carried its arms at its sides, as people do, its hands would drag along the ground. But the hoolock holds its arms over its head as it runs. This stance helps the hoolock keep its balance. Like other gibbons, the hoolock is a master at traveling through trees. It swings with grace and confidence from one branch to another.

The hoolock gibbon does not grasp a branch with its hands. Instead, it uses its hands as hooks, briefly supporting its body without stopping its swift movement. It also makes long leaps from one branch to another. Indeed, a hoolock can travel faster through the treetops than a person can run on the ground. Rapid escape is the hoolock's main defense against such enemies as leopards and snakes.

The fur coat of a hoolock is dense and shaggy. Young hoolocks and adult males have black fur with white markings. Adult females have light yellow-brown fur. Hoolocks live in small groups consisting of a male, a female, and their children. Usually one baby is born at a time. The baby clings tightly to its mother as she moves through the trees. The mother often uses her legs or one arm to cradle the baby so that it does not fall. Hoolocks sleep sitting up on high branches. Usually they choose branches that extend farthest from the trunk. If a leopard or snake tries to reach them, the branch shakes and the hoolocks have time to escape.

Giraffe
Giraffa camelopardalis

Length: 13 to 15 feet
Height to Top of Head: up to 18 feet
Weight: 1,200 to 4,300 pounds
Diet: leaves and branches of trees, mostly acacias

Number of Young: 1
Home: savannas of Africa south of the Sahara
Order: even-toed hoofed mammals
Family: giraffes, okapis

  Grasslands

Mammals

© MARTIN HARVEY / CORBIS

Most herds of giraffe live in the East African savanna. This area is south of the Sahara Desert. It is the home of the "reticulated" giraffe. This giraffe gets its name from the design of its coat. It is a network of white lines and large brown patches. The reticulated giraffe grows to 16 feet.

Giraffes graze on tree leaves and small branches. They prefer the leaves of acacias and wild apricot trees. The giraffe first catches a branch in its mouth. It then pulls back its head to get a mouthful of leaves. Giraffes can eat more than 65 pounds of leaves and twigs a day!

The giraffe has little to fear in the savanna. It is a very fast runner. A kick from one of its large hooves can even kill a lion. Its enemies usually attack only baby giraffes. But an adult giraffe can be attacked when it takes a drink. To reach the water, it must spread its front legs. In this position it cannot defend itself. It takes a giraffe quite a while to stand upright again. And during this time it is open to attack.

Giraffes have a peaceful nature. Even when males fight, the winner never chases the loser. When the fight is over, the two males rub muzzles. They then rest together.

Brindled Gnu (Wildebeest)
Connochaetes taurinus

Length: 6 to 7 feet
Height: 4 to 5 feet
Weight: 350 to 500 pounds
Diet: grasses and leaves of small plants
Number of Young: 1

Home: southern Africa
Order: even-toed hoofed mammals
Family: antelope, bison, buffalo, cattle, goats, and sheep

 Grasslands

 Mammals

© MARTIN HARVEY / CORBIS

The male gnu's head, with its curved horns, looks like a bull's head. But its tail and mane make you think of a horse. The gnu looks different from either cows or horses. It has a large beard that makes it look like an old man. This is especially true of gnus in South Africa. They have white beards. Those from eastern Africa have black beards.

The gnu is a member of the cow family. It is a great runner and can travel long distances. It can even reach speeds of up to 50 miles per hour. It protects itself from lions, leopards, cheetahs, and hyenas by outrunning them. A newborn gnu can stand and run when it's only five minutes old!

Male and female gnus live apart in herds of up to 1,000 animals. In the grassy African savanna, huge herds of gnus mix with zebras. When they are three or four years old, male gnus start to leave the herd and find their own territories. There are rarely serious fights between males over these territories. They usually just push each other, horns against horns. The winner is allowed to mate with females that enter the territory.

In the dry season, gnus take long trips looking for water and grasses. Thousands die of exhaustion during these trips. Gnus are hunted for their leather. Their numbers have declined in recent years. But large herds are still found in eastern Africa.

Goldfish
Carassius auratus

Length: 2 inches to 1 foot
Diet: small plants and food matter
Number of Eggs: 500 to 1,000

Home: Eurasia, North America, and Australia
Order: minnows, suckers
Family: carps and minnows

 Freshwater

Fish

© MICHAEL KELLER / CORBIS

Wild goldfish are about a foot long. They are dull brown in color. They all look very much the same. But there are more than 120 different kinds of domesticated goldfish. And they come in a stunning variety of shapes, sizes, and colors. They can be 2 inches long or 1 foot long. They can be red, blue, orange, yellow, black, white, or any combination of these colors. The most common color is orange. Some breeds have large, bulbous eyes and rounded bellies. An example is the black moor. Others, like the fantail, have long, oversized fins.

Why are there so many different kinds of domesticated goldfish? Why are they so much more beautiful than wild ones? They were bred to look this way. The Chinese have been breeding goldfish for more than a thousand years. Goldfish are originally from East Asia. Over the years they have traveled to other parts of the world. They can be found in freshwater streams and ponds in Europe, North America, and Australia. Spring and summer is the time for breeding. Females lay between 500 and 1,000 eggs at a time. The tiny eggs stick to vegetation. A week later baby goldfish hatch. They are called fry. They feed from a yolk sac for two days. Then they swim on their own.

In the wild, goldfish live about 15 years. They can survive almost as long in captivity. They are widely farmed and kept as pets in aquariums.

Canada Goose
Branta canadensis

Length: 22 to 48 inches
Wingspan: up to 6 feet
Diet: omnivorous
Number of Eggs: 4 to 6
Home: North America, British Isles, and Scandinavia

Order: ducks, geese, swans, waterfowl
Family: ducks, geese, and swans

 Freshwater

 Birds

© JULIE HABEL / CORBIS

Most North American Canada geese live in Alaska and Canada during the summer. They fly south at the beginning of winter. They do this to get away from the cold weather and to look for new sources of food. They fly across the United States to warmer areas. Their destinations are California and the southern Midwest, northern Mexico, and southern Florida. And they settle along the Atlantic coast. They follow four main routes south. But many Canada geese now live all year in the northeastern part of the United States. Unlike the birds that fly south, these "permanent" geese are rarely hunted. But they are not always welcome guests. They like the lawns and ponds of golf courses, large homes, and college campuses. There they leave their droppings, eat the grass, and dig up roots and tubers. In the spring and summer, they also feed on insect larvae, worms, small mollusks, and shellfish. The Canada goose was brought from England about 250 years ago.

Canada geese form couples that often stay together for life. The partners build a nest together. The nest is usually in a calm marshy area. There it is hidden by plants and trees. They make the nest by weaving together grasses, stems, and leaves. The nest is shaped like a shallow bowl. The inside is lined with goose down, threads, and animal hair. The female lays four to six eggs. She sits on them to keep them warm. The male stands guard and protects them. When the chicks are about two months old, they learn to fly.

Snow Goose
Anser caerulescens

Length: 25 to 31 inches
Wingspan: 53 to 60 inches
Weight: 5½ to 7½ pounds
Diet: roots, grasses, grain, and other plant matter
Number of Eggs: 3 to 8

Home: Greenland, North America, and Asia
Order: ducks, geese, swans, waterfowl
Family: ducks, geese, and swans

Arctic and Antarctic

Birds

© WINFRIED WISNIEWSKI / ZEFA / CORBIS

During the short Arctic summer, snow geese gather by the thousands in flat, marshy areas. There they build nests, one right next to another, as far as the eye can see. In such close quarters, the snow geese must be very protective of their nests and their young. In fact, while the female incubates the eggs, her mate spends nearly all his time guarding her. The parents lovingly care for their young, which begin to fly about 40 days after they hatch.

As summer ends, an internal clock inside the snow goose seems to "click." The bird begins to eat constantly, becoming quite fat. Soon it begins to migrate southward, joining a flock that flies in long, wavy lines. People on the ground may hear the birds' high-pitched honking. Many snow geese that summer in northern Canada fly to the Gulf Coast of the United States—a distance of some 1,700 miles. By the time the snow goose arrives at its winter grounds, it has burned up most of the weight it gained before the journey. In spring the snow goose returns to the Arctic. Flocks return year after year to the same breeding grounds.

There are two kinds, or subspecies, of snow goose: the greater snow goose and the lesser snow goose. The greater snow goose is all white except for black wing tips. The lesser snow goose has two color phases. In its white phase, it looks like the greater snow goose. In its blue phase, it has blue gray wings.

Gorilla
Gorilla gorilla

Height: up to 6 feet
Weight: 175 to 200 pounds (female); 300 to 400 pounds (male)
Diet: mostly leaves and shoots

Number of Young: 1
Home: West and Central Africa
Order: primates
Family: great apes

Rain Forests

Mammals

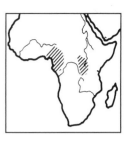

© JORG & PETRA WEGNER / ANIMALS ANIMALS / EARTH SCENES

Endangered Animals

Few other animals have been the subject of as many legends as the gorilla. However, it isn't the man-eating monster that many people imagine. In fact, it eats nothing but leaves, fruits, and plant sources.

Gorillas live in groups of 2 to 30. The groups are territorial. A territory can be as large as 12 square miles. The group, or family, is highly structured. It is headed by a dominant male. He is usually the largest and strongest. There are 2 to 3 smaller males in the group. Several females and young gorillas of all ages complete the family. Gorillas travel slowly through the forest. They move no more than half a mile a day. They leave behind them a powerful scent that can be detected from 150 feet. Gorillas spend nearly 15 hours a day sleeping. Each night they build their nests out of branches. Gorillas are shy animals. They charge only when they are taken by surprise. Even then, they charge to hide their fear.

There are two subspecies of gorillas. These are the lowland gorilla and the mountain gorilla. Lowland gorillas live in the forests of several African countries. These include Cameroon, Gabon, the Central African Republic, Congo, and Zaire. Mountain gorillas live in the mountains separating East and Central Africa. The number of gorillas is decreasing. There are now only several thousand left. They are legally protected. But illegal hunting and loss of natural habitat continue to destroy them.

Evening Grosbeak
Coccothraustes vespertinus

Length: about 8 inches
Weight: 1½ to 3 ounces
Diet: seeds, fruits, and insects
Number of Eggs: 3 or 4

Home: North America
Order: perching birds
Family: buntings, finches

 Forests and Mountains

 Birds

© TIM ZUROWSKI / CORBIS

As their name suggests, evening grosbeaks are often seen at dusk. In winter, these yellow finches swarm around feeding trays in large numbers. They are surprisingly unafraid of humans. Originally a western bird, the species has been spreading eastward for the past 100 years.

The evening grosbeak has the advantage of being able to eat a wide variety of foods. In the western mountains, the bird eats mainly piñon nuts and juniper berries. But in the east, it feasts on maple sap and the buds of leafy trees. In the fall, all grosbeaks eat lots of seeds. In the summer, adult grosbeaks also catch insects. Parent birds mash the bugs into a high-protein baby food for their chicks. Finally, grosbeaks add minerals and salt to their diet by eating small amounts of dirt and gravel.

Like most North American birds, evening grosbeaks breed in April, May, and June. How does the courting male catch the attention of a mate? He bows low, fluffs up his feathers, and then quivers his wings.

After mating, the female builds a loose nest of twigs, usually far out on a limb. She lines the nest with feathers and other soft materials and lays several pretty blue green eggs. As the mother bird sits on her eggs, her mate brings her food. When the chicks hatch, they keep both parents busy with their noisy demands for food.

Rose-breasted Grosbeak
Pheucticus ludovicianus

Length: 7½ inches
Weight: less than 1½ ounces
Diet: seeds and insects
Number of Eggs: 2 to 5
Home: northeastern North America, Central America, and South America

Order: perching birds
Family: buntings, finches

Forests and Mountains

Birds

© MARIE READ / ANIMALS ANIMALS / EARTH SCENES

The rose-breasted grosbeak is one of many species of cardinals known for bright colors and lively songs. It is the colorful male who gives this species its name. Its breast is red, the head and upper parts are black, and the underside is white. The female is actually quite drab, with a brown head and white breast. The grosbeak's sweet song has many versions, a different one for each area in which the bird is found.

Male rose-breasted grosbeaks begin the mating season trying to attract females. They do this with an odd courtship dance of quick movements and peculiar poses. When a male has won a female's attention, they will mate. They join forces to build a cup-shaped nest that will eventually hold as many as five eggs. The mother and father take turns sitting on the eggs and share the job of finding insect larvae to feed to their young. In fact, the grosbeak's appetite for these harmful insect pests is a great help to gardeners and farmers.

By the middle of October, families of rose-breasted grosbeaks are ready to migrate. They will travel to warmer climates for the winter. Many end up in Peru and Venezuela. Once in their winter vacation spot, the grosbeaks reside in alpine meadows or near farms and open forests. They head back home in March, returning to their breeding grounds in May.

Guinea Pig
Cavia porcellus

Length: about 10 inches
Weight: 1 to 2 pounds
Diet: grasses, hay, leaves, bark, fruits, roots, blossoms, and seeds

Number of Young: 1 to 4
Home: worldwide
Order: rodents
Family: cavies

 Cities, Towns, and Farms

 Mammals

© HAND REINHARD / ZEFA / CORBIS

The guinea pig is a popular and gentle children's pet. It was domesticated 3,000 to 6,000 years ago. Villagers in the mountains of Peru tamed the wild cavy. This was the guinea pig's ancestor. They kept the wild cavy around their huts. It was fattened on garbage, then killed and eaten. In fact, it was a favorite meal of the ancient Peruvians. Today guinea pigs are still raised as farm animals in various parts of Central and South America.

In the 16th century, traders brought a cargo of domestic guinea pigs to Europe. They immediately became popular pets. The guinea pig shares many traits with the wild cavy. There are differences, however. The guinea pig is calmer and gentler around humans. It also purrs like a cat. The adult males purr loudly and often. The females and piglets have a softer purr. They also don't purr as much.

Guinea pigs have long, sharp teeth. But they rarely bite their owners. They are easy to care for. They thrive on common foods. These include oat flakes, apples, lettuce, and carrots. Pet guinea pigs breed easily. They also mate throughout the year. Newborn piglets emerge fully developed. Their eyes and ears are open. Guinea pigs may live to seven years of age.

More than a fine pet, guinea pigs are important laboratory animals. Believe it or not, the guinea pig's anatomy is a lot like a human's. That is why they are used in various types of medical and drug research.

Laughing Gull
Larus atricilla

Length: 15 to 17 inches
Wingspan: about 42 inches
Diet: mainly small fish; also tern eggs and earthworms
Number of Eggs: 3 or 4
Home: coastal areas in North, Central, and South America

Order: auks, herons, and relatives
Family: gulls, puffins, terns, and relatives

Oceans and Shores

Birds

© ARTHUR MORRIS / CORBIS

This gull's method of catching fish is no laughing matter! The laughing gull will see a brown pelican with fish hanging from its pouch. It will land on the pelican's head and grab one of the fish. Jaegers and frigate birds play similar tricks on the gull. They chase the gull through the air. This forces it to drop its food. The gull also feeds on fish that it catches on the ocean's surface. The bird circles until it spots food. The gull then dive-bombs toward the water. It picks up the food in its bill.

The laughing gull is named for its calls. One call sounds like "hah-ha-ha-ha-hah-hah-hah." Another call is "ka-ha, ka-ha." Adult males and females look alike. Their plumage, however, changes with the seasons. In summer a laughing gull has a black head. In winter its head is white with gray spots.

Most birds migrate with the seasons. So does the laughing gull. In summer it lives as far north as Nova Scotia. It flies south along coasts, spending the winter in the warmer climates of the southern United States. It may even go as far south as Central America and South America.

Laughing gulls nest in colonies on coastal islands. They can also be found along beaches and in marshes. Their large, ground-level nest is made of grasses and reeds. The parents incubate the eggs for about 20 days. Newborn laughing gull chicks are covered with soft down. The babies receive food that has been partly digested by their parents.

Guppy
Poecilia reticulata

Length: up to 2 inches
Diet: aquatic insects, algae, and fish eggs
Number of Young: 10 to 100
Home: native to the West Indies and northern South America; introduced elsewhere

Order: killifishes
Family: live-bearers, livebearing toothcarps

 Freshwater

 Fish

© GERARD LACZ / PETER ARNOLD, INC.

The guppy is one of the best-known aquarium fish in the world. Why is it such an easy fish to keep? Because it doesn't mind small changes in water temperature. The guppy matures rapidly. It also produces large quantities of eggs. For these reasons, guppies are used in science laboratories. They are used in experiments in genetics, fish physiology, and breeding behavior.

Guppies also serve humans in other ways. They help control malaria outbreaks. How can guppies fight a human disease? They eat the floating larvae of the mosquitoes. These insects carry the malaria germ. If you reduce the number of mosquitoes, fewer people will get malaria. In this way, the guppies have saved thousands of human lives. They have been sent to Argentina, Hawaii, and Singapore for this purpose.

Most fish lay eggs, but guppies are viviparous. This means they give birth to live young. The first thing a newly born guppy does is swim to the surface. There it gulps air to fill its swim bladder. This helps the baby guppy swim. And it had better swim fast.

Guppy mothers will eat their own young. Fish breeders prevent this from happening. The place their pregnant guppies in "maternity cages." These cages have holes big enough to let the babies escape. The holes are small enough to keep their mothers at bay.

Common Hamster
Cricetus cricetus

Length of the Body: 8 to 11 inches
Length of the Tail: 2 to 2¾ inches
Weight: ¾ to 16 ounces
Diet: seeds, plants, and small animals

Number of Young: 4 to 11
Home: central Eurasia
Order: rodents
Family: mice, rats

 Cities, Towns, and Farms

 Mammals

© SYLVAIN CORDIER / BIOS / PETER ARNOLD, INC.

The common hamster is about twice the size of a pet, or "golden," hamster. The common hamster is also more colorful. It has calico fur of yellow, red, and brown. It also has bright white hands and a handsome black belly. Like all hamsters, this species has expandable cheek pouches on either side of its mouth. The animal can stuff its cheeks with a large amount of food.

Common hamsters live in the farm fields of central Europe and Russia. When the hamster population is booming, this little rodent can be a serious pest. It steals grain, corn, potatoes, and beets. The common hamster also eats meat. It is large and fierce enough to kill other rodents, such as mice. It also dines on small birds. Usually the hamster hauls its food back to its underground den for storage.

The den of a young common hamster is a simple home. A long, downward-slanting tunnel leads to a nesting chamber. There is also a food-storage room. As it gets older, the hamster enlarges its home. It adds a second tunnel for emergency escapes. Several dead-end tunnels are built to trap small animals. The hamster also digs extra food chambers. It stuffs these with grain and vegetables.

In October, common hamsters prepare to hibernate. Before curling up for a winter's sleep, each hamster crams its cheek pouches with food. It may wake up every few days to nibble. But it won't emerge from its den until spring.

Snowshoe Hare
Lepus americanus

Length: 20 inches
Weight: 3 pounds
Diet: grass, bark, and weeds
Number of Young: 2 to 5
Home: Canada and the northern United States

Order: hares, pikas, and rabbits
Family: hares, rabbits

 Forests and Mountains

 Mammals

© TOM BRAKEFIELD / CORBIS

The snowshoe hare changes the color of its coat to match the season. In order to hide from foxes and lynx, the hare wears a brown coat during the summer. This blends in well with trees and soil. In winter the hare turns white to blend in with the snow. But the snowshoe hare doesn't turn white all at once. The first part of its body to change is its feet. So, for a short time, it looks as though the hare is wearing snowshoes.

The snowshoe hare has babies as often as four times a year. The young hares are known as leverets. They have to fend for themselves during the day because their mother is busy looking for food. At twilight, she visits her babies so they can nurse. But then they are back on their own again. Scientists have found that fewer than a quarter of leverets survive their first year.

The snowshoe hare goes through dramatic population booms and busts every 8 to 12 years. The population "booms" because these hares breed rapidly. At the same time, the hare's predators increase in number thanks to the abundance of hares to eat! Eventually the snowshoe-hare population gets so large that it runs out of plants to eat. The hares starve and die off rapidly. The predators that depend on them for food likewise starve to death. The whole cycle begins again once the plants that the hare eats have a chance to regrow.

Great Blue Heron
Ardea herodias

Length: 3 to 4½ feet
Wingspan: up to 7 feet
Diet: fish and small animals
Number of Eggs: 3 to 7
Home: North America, West Indies, Central America, northern coast of South America

Order: auks, herons, and relatives
Family: bitterns, egrets

 Freshwater

 Birds

© D. ROBERT & LORRI FRANZ / CORBIS

The great blue heron is well named. Its grayish back sometimes seems blue. The heron is found near lakes and alongside rivers. Other habitats are the seashores of the Atlantic and Pacific oceans. Herons prefer shallow water. They will spend hours there fishing. Sometimes the great blue heron is completely white. It is often called the great white egret. But it is really a heron. It is white because it lives on a marine diet.

Fish is a diet staple of the great blue heron. When fishing, the blue heron is very patient. It waits for the fish to come. It then stabs it with its powerful beak. It also eats frogs, salamanders, and snakes. Crabs, shrimp, and crayfish are also part of its diet. This bird also hunts on land. There it will capture snakes, lizards, and large insects.

Another food source is fish farms. Both blue and gray herons will fish there.

The great blue heron builds its nest in a tall tree. It often selects one in the middle of the woods. This is where it lays its eggs. It may use the same nest for several years in a row. The heron sits on the eggs for 28 days. The parents take turns doing this. Blue herons are a lot like other herons, egrets, and bitterns. They live in colonies. There may be 150 or more couples in a colony. When the young are hatched, the noise is deafening!

Not all great blue herons migrate. Herons in the southern part of the United States are one example. Herons of the north migrate to Central America and the West Indies. Some go as far as the extreme northeast coast of South America.

Green-Backed Heron
Butorides striatus

Length: 15 to 19 inches
Wingspan: 20 to 24 inches
Diet: mainly fish
Number of Eggs: 2 to 4
Home: South America, Africa, Asia, Polynesia, and Australia

Order: auks, herons, and relatives
Family: bitterns, egrets

Freshwater

Birds

© JOE MCDONALD / CORBIS

Night has fallen over the mangrove forest. This is a dense growth of trees and shrubs common along tropical rivers and seashores. At the edges of the water lurks a green-backed heron. Suddenly the heron lunges into the water. It spears a fish with its bill. Another heron flying overhead also spots food and dives into the water. This scene is repeated over and over again as these birds search for food. The green-backed heron always looks hungry. Indeed, when the food supply is plentiful, it is a greedy eater. Mainly fish, but also frogs, crabs, mollusks, insects, and worms make up its diet.

The green-backed heron is a thin bird with long legs, a long neck, and a pointed bill. It usually stays in the same area all year. But some may migrate when the rains stop and the ground dries up. In flight a heron usually folds its neck so that its head is tucked back to the shoulders. The legs stretch backward, trailing behind the body. The heron is an excellent flyer. It moves easily and surely among the mangrove trees. Both parents incubate the eggs and care for the babies in a nest made from twigs.

In some places the green-backed heron is a shy, secretive creature. During the day, it rests in tall grass and under overhanging branches, flying at sundown to look for food. Herons that live near city ponds and mud banks are accustomed to people and will often feed during the day.

Atlantic Herring
Clupea harengus

Length: up to 18 inches
Diet: copepods, mollusks, and other small invertebrates
Number of Eggs: 10,000 to 50,000

Home: North Atlantic Ocean
Order: anchovies, herrings
Family: herrings

 Oceans and Shores

 Fish

© HINRICH BAESEMANN / DPA / CORBIS

The Atlantic herring is one of the most important fish in the world. Each year, fishermen catch many tons of Atlantic herring. Some are sold for bait or used to make oils, fertilizers, and other products. The rest are processed and eaten by people. Millions of young herring are sold as sardines. The Atlantic herring is also an important member of ocean food chains. It feeds on small organisms that it strains from the water with long, comb like rakers on the edges of its gills. In turn the herring and its eggs are eaten by other kinds of fish and by seabirds.

The Atlantic herring spends most of its life in deep water far from shore. At breeding time, it gathers with other herring into enormous groups, or schools. Together they move toward coasts to spawn (lay eggs). The eggs are small and heavily covered with mucus. They sink to the seafloor, where masses of them stick to seaweed and stones. The eggs hatch in 8 to 40 days, depending on the water temperature. The Atlantic herring has a long life span. It sometimes survives for 20 years. However, most Atlantic herring are caught by humans or other predators long before they reach this age. There are about 100 species of herring in addition to the Atlantic variety. Among them is the Pacific herring, which lives in the North Pacific Ocean. It is very similar to the Atlantic herring.

Hippopotamus
Hippopotamus amphibius

Length: 10 to 11½ feet
Weight: 3,000 to 7,000 pounds
Diet: herbivorous
Number of Young: 1

Home: tropical Africa
Order: even-toed hoofed
  mammals
Family: hippopotamuses

 Grasslands

 Mammals

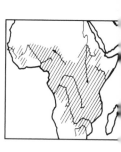

© PETER JOHNSON / CORBIS

The hippopotamus, or "hippo," spends most of the day sleeping on river shores. But it also enters the water and lies there without moving. It does this to escape the strong African sun. Only its eyes and nostrils may appear above the surface. It looks like a submarine periscope. The hippo is also a good swimmer and diver. It can stay underwater for three to five minutes. It closes its ears and nostrils while underwater.

The skin of the hippopotamus produces an oily liquid. This protects the hippo's skin. The oil screens out the sun's drying rays. It also prevents water damage from the hippo's long stays in the water. The small drops of this liquid have a reddish sheen. It was once believed that the hippopotamus was sweating blood.

In mating season, the males are sometimes seen in violent combat. Each one will try to plant its large canine teeth into the body of its rival. At that time, hippos may also attack canoes. But they generally do not bother people. Mating takes place in shallow water. A young hippopotamus can only be nursed underwater. It escapes crocodiles by taking refuge on its mother's back.

The hippopotamus is a source of valuable products. It has been hunted for its meat, fat, and leather. Hunters even sought the ivory from its teeth. For this reason, the hippopotamus has become rare in West and South Africa. Many still live along the rivers of East Africa. Its closest relative is the pygmy hippopotamus. It lives in the forests of West Africa.

Pygmy Hippopotamus
Hexaprotodon liberiensis

Length: up to 60 inches
Length of the Tail: 11 inches
Height at the Shoulder: 30 inches
Weight: 400 to 500 pounds
Diet: various plant matter

Number of Young: 1
Home: West Africa
Order: even-toed hoofed mammals
Family: hippopotamuses

 Rain Forests

 Mammals

© MARTIN HARVEY / CORBIS

The Romans called the hippopotamus an "African water pig." This wasn't a bad name because hippos are related to pigs. With their chunky build and big belly, they even look like pigs.

Pygmy hippos are shy creatures. They avoid open spaces, people, and other animals. They live in dense, swampy forests. And they spend most of the day in special resting places at the edge of swamps or streams. They move about and feed in late afternoon and at night. Pygmy hippos may be almost invisible in the dark. But it isn't very difficult to track them down. They are very noisy eaters. As they chew on grass and other plants, they can be heard from a distance of 150 feet or more.

Over and over again, as they move through the forest, pygmy hippos travel along the same routes. Over a period of time, well-marked "hippo paths" form. Pygmy hippos are good swimmers. But they do not spend as much time in the water as their larger hippo cousins. If chased by a predator, they try to escape into dense thickets rather than into water. Also, unlike large hippos, pygmy hippos live alone or in pairs. They never live in herds.

The pygmy hippo's dark brown, hairless skin is a couple of inches thick. Special glands in the skin produce a sticky, reddish brown secretion. This secretion, like a person's sweat, helps to remove excess heat from the hippo's body.

Great Hornbill
Buceros bicornis

Length: about 47 inches, including an 11-inch beak
Diet: fruit, insects, and other small animals

Number of Eggs: usually 2
Home: Southeast Asia
Order: hornbills and relatives
Family: hornbills

Rain Forests

Birds

© MICHAEL SEWELL / PETER ARNOLD, INC.

The great hornbill sports an enormous beak, which is topped by a helmet called a casque. Fortunately, the casque is hollow and the beak contains many air chambers. If these structures were solid, they would be very heavy, and the great hornbill would be unable to fly.

Hornbills have unique nesting habits. After a male and female court and mate, the female enters a hole in a tree. There she lays her eggs and raises her young. She closes the entrance to the hole by building a wall from materials brought to her by the male: a mixture of mud and excrement. Only a very small "window," just big enough for the tip of the male's beak, is left. The wall helps protect the female and her babies from snakes, monkeys, and other predators. The window is used to pass food into the hole. In the following weeks, while the female great hornbill incubates the eggs and cares for the babies, her mate brings food a dozen or more times a day. When the young birds are ready to leave the nest, the female uses her beak to break down the wall.

Great hornbills are noisy birds. They leap from tree to tree, often catching insects in the air. In the morning and evening, they may descend to the forest floor, where they hop about looking for food or a place to bathe. Males and females are difficult to tell apart because they have similar plumage. But the iris of a male's eye is red, while that of a female's eye is white.

Rhinoceros Hornbill
Buceros rhinoceros

Height: 48 inches (male); 36 inches (female)
Diet: fruits, insects, lizards, and small mammals
Number of Eggs: 1 to 3

Home: Sumatra and southern Malayan Peninsula
Order: hornbills and relatives
Family: hornbills

Rain Forests

Birds

© GERALD CUBITT / NHPA

Echoing through the mountain mist, in the thick rain forest of Sumatra, comes the sound of a distant freight train. One might expect to hear a train whistle blow. Instead, the sound that follows is a loud, deep "GR-RONK!" This is no train, but rather a huge rhinoceros hornbill. This bird has a horny growth on its enormous beak. It amplifies the sound of its call. To counterbalance the weight of its beak, the hornbill has developed long, broad tail feathers.

The rhinoceros hornbill is among the largest of the 44 species in the hornbill family. It is also one of the least known. Why? Because it lives in remote jungle highlands. The spectacular red horn on its beak is lighter in weight than it looks. It is a honeycomb of bony tissue encased in a thin, but strong, shell.

Hornbills mate for life, and the female depends greatly on her mate's devotion. Female hornbills literally wall themselves into their nest holes with mud when it is time to lay their eggs. In this way the mother and her nestlings keep safe from the many snakes and other predators that prowl the rain forest. However, this leaves the female hornbill entirely dependent on her mate. He feeds her and her chicks through a small hole in the mud wall. What happens when the father hornbill can no longer keep up with his family's growing appetite? His mate and their half-grown chicks break free.

American Horsefly
Tabanus americanus

Length: ¾ to 1 inch
Diet: blood of warm-blooded animals (female); nectar (male)
Method of Reproduction: egg layer

Home: North America
Order: gnats, mosquitoes, true flies
Family: clegs, deer flies, horseflies

 Cities, Towns, and Farms

 Arthropods

© JEFFREY LEPORE / PHOTO RESEARCHERS

The female American horsefly loves warmth, sunlight, and blood! This fly attacks horses and cattle. Large animals can't outrun this pesky insect. It is a powerful flier. And it can chase an animal a long way.

When the horsefly bites, it puts saliva in the wound. There is a chemical in the saliva. This chemical does not allow the bleeding to stop. The fly then licks and sucks the blood. The wound keeps bleeding even after the fly stops feeding. So a horse or cow can lose a lot of blood.

Most American horseflies live near their breeding grounds. They are found in swamps, marshes, ponds, streams, and lakes. The female places her eggs on plants that grow over water. When the eggs hatch, the larvae fall into the water. They eat small animals that live in the water. First they bury their head deep into a victim. Then they suck out the body juices.

The larvae spend two winters buried in mud at the bottom of the water. Then they enter the pupa stage and become adults. Male American horseflies live just a few weeks. Females live through the spring and summer. They die when cool weather arrives in the fall.

Broad-tailed Hummingbird
Selasphorus platycercus

Length: 4 to 4½ inches
Diet: nectar, tree sap, small insects, and spiders
Number of Eggs: 2
Home: *Summer:* Rocky Mountains west to California

Winter: Mexico and Guatemala
Order: hummingbirds, swifts
Family: hummingbirds

 Forests and Mountains

 Birds

© RON SANFORD / CORBIS

In springtime, you can find broad-tailed hummingbirds flying high over Rocky Mountain meadows. They have a wild courtship dance. Like bright jewels in the sky, a pair of broad-tailed hummingbirds will skyrocket 90 feet in the air, one following 4 to 5 feet below the other. Then the tiny pair descend side by side, only to shoot skyward again.

You can tell this species of American hummingbird from others by the shrill buzzing whistle it makes when flying forward. The sound is created by air rushing through slots in the bird's wing tips. During breeding season the male broad-tailed hummingbird uses his flight whistle to scare other males away from his courtship territory.

After broad-tailed hummingbirds mate, the couple build a tiny cup-shaped nest on the limb of a branch. Often they place the nest over a refreshing mountain stream. They love to bathe in the splashing water. The birds weave their nest out of fluffy plant down and silk from spiderwebs and cocoons.

Like most hummingbirds, broadtails drink flower nectar. Their favorite is the nectar of scarlet gilias. These flowers grow in high mountain meadows. They must drink nearly their weight in nectar each day because they burn a lot of calories with their furious flying. For protein and fat, hummingbirds eat small spiders and insects.

Ruby-throated Hummingbird
Archilochus colubris

Length: 3½ inches
Diet: flower nectar and insects
Number of Eggs: 2

Home: North America
Order: hummingbirds, swifts
Family: hummingbirds

Cities, Towns, and Farms

Birds

Fourteen species of hummingbirds breed in North America. Of these, only the ruby-throated hummingbird is found east of the Mississippi River. It is frequently seen in gardens, feeding from tubular red flowers. It also likes bird feeders filled with a mixture of honey and sugar water. It is one of the smallest birds in the United States.

Both the male and female of this species have iridescent green feathers on the upper part of their bodies. The male is distinguished by his bright upper feather and his ruby-red throat. The female's throat is white. The female builds the nest high in the branches of a tree. She uses lichen, ferns, soft grass, or dandelion-seed down bound together with cobwebs. The female usually lays two small white eggs. These hatch two weeks later. In about three weeks, the young birds have grown their flight feathers and are ready to leave the nest.

In flight the wings of the ruby-throated hummingbird appear to be a blur. This bird hovers almost motionless while feeding on nectar. Its wings flap at an amazing 55 beats per second. Despite its small size, the ruby-throated hummingbird migrates great distances. It travels across the Gulf of Mexico to Central America for the winter. The hummingbird prepares for the long journey across the gulf. It stores up enough fat to increase its weight by 50 percent.

A

aardvark **1**:5
acorn woodpecker **10**:37
Adelie penguin **7**:18
African bullfrog **2**:11
African elephant **3**:36
African wild ass **1**:18
Alabama water dog **10**:17
albatross, wandering **1**:6
alligator, American **1**:7
alpine ibex **5**:7
Amazon dolphin **3**:21
American alligator **1**:7
American anhinga **1**:10
American bison **1**:37
American bumblebee **2**:12
American cockroach **2**:37
American horsefly **4**:42
American lobster **5**:34
American marten **6**:6
American mink **6**:8
American robin **7**:44
American toad **9**:32
amphibians
    bullfrog **2**:10
    bullfrog, African **2**:11
    frog, Cuban tree **4**:13
    frog, green **4**:14
    frog, poison dart **4**:15
    frog, wood **4**:16
    peeper, spring **7**:17
    toad, American **9**:32
    toad, western spadefoot **9**:33
    water dog, Alabama **10**:17
anaconda, green **1**:8
Andean condor **2**:39
angelfish **1**:9
anhinga, American **1**:10
ant, army **1**:11
ant, black carpenter **1**:12
ant, fire **1**:13
anteater, giant **1**:14
ant-eating woodpecker (acorn
    woodpecker) **10**:37
Arabian camel **2**:16
Arabian oryx **6**:37
archerfish **1**:15
Arctic char **2**:24
Arctic fox **4**:9
Arctic ground squirrel **9**:8
Arctic tern **9**:25
armadillo, screaming hairy **1**:16
armadillo lizard **5**:31
army ant **1**:11
arthropods
    ant, army **1**:11
    ant, black carpenter **1**:12
    ant, fire **1**:13
    bed bug **1**:32
    bee, honey **1**:33
    beetle, Japanese **1**:34
    bumblebee, American **2**:12
    butterfly, monarch **2**:13
    caterpillar, woolly bear **2**:22
    centipede, house **2**:23
    cicada, seventeen-year **2**:30
    cockroach, American **2**:37
    crab, Florida stone **3**:6
    crab, giant hermit **3**:7
    crab, horseshoe **3**:8
    cricket, house **3**:11
    daddy longlegs (harvestman)
        3:14
    fiddler, Atlantic marsh **3**:41
    firefly, North American **3**:42
    fly, tsetse **4**:8
    fruit fly, common **4**:7
    horsefly, American **4**:42
    lobster, American **5**:34
    lobster, Caribbean spiny **5**:35
    mantis, praying **5**:44
    mosquito **6**:22
    moth, Atlas **6**:23
    moth, gypsy **6**:24
    moth, luna **6**:25
    nymph, common wood **6**:31
    shrimp, common **8**:32
    shrimp, northern pink **8**:33
    spider, black widow **8**:44
    spider, garden **9**:5
    spider, house **9**:6
    spider, wolf **9**:7
    tarantula **9**:21
    tarantula, desert blond **9**:22
    termite, eastern subterranean
        9:24
    water bug, giant **10**:16
    weevil, boll **10**:19
    yellow jacket, eastern **10**:42
Asian cobra **2**:34
Asian dhole **3**:18
Asian elephant **3**:37
Asiatic black bear **1**:28
asp **1**:17
ass, African wild **1**:18
Atlantic herring **4**:37
Atlantic marsh fiddler **3**:41
Atlantic puffin **7**:29
Atlantic razor clam **2**:31
Atlantic salmon **8**:6
Atlantic stingray **9**:13
Atlantic walrus **10**:12
Atlas moth **6**:23
aye-aye **1**:19

B

baboons
    chacma **1**:20
    gelada **1**:21
    hamadryas **1**:22
    yellow **1**:23
Bactrian camel **2**:17
badger, Eurasian **1**:24
bald eagle **3**:32
ball python **7**:31
banded linsang **5**:29
banded mongoose **6**:11
bandicoot, spiny **1**:25
Barbary macaque **5**:38
barn owl **6**:42
barn swallow **9**:15
barracuda, great **1**:26
bass, striped **1**:27
bay scallop **8**:12
bearded pig **7**:24
bearded seal **8**:18
bears
    Asiatic black **1**:28
    black **1**:29
    brown **1**:30
    panda, giant **7**:9
    panda, red **7**:10
    polar **1**:31
bed bug **1**:32
bee, honey **1**:33
beetle, Japanese **1**:34
beluga **1**:35
Bengal tiger **9**:28
bighorn sheep **8**:31
bird-eating spider (tarantula) **9**:21
bird of paradise, blue **1**:36
birds
    albatross, wandering **1**:6
    anhinga, American **1**:10
    blackbird, red-winged **1**:38
    bluebird, eastern **1**:39
    bluebird, mountain **1**:40
    blue bird of paradise **1**:36
    bobolink **2**:5
    booby, masked **2**:7
    booby, red-footed **2**:8
    bufflehead **2**:9
    buzzard, common **2**:14
    cardinal **2**:20
    cockatiel **2**:35
    cockatoo, sulphur-crested **2**:36
    condor, Andean **2**:39
    condor, California **2**:40
    crane, common **3**:9
    crane, whooping **3**:10
    dove, white-winged **3**:27
    duck, mandarin **3**:29
    duck, ruddy **3**:30
    duck, wood **3**:31
    eagle, bald **3**:32
    egret, snowy **3**:35
    falcon, peregrine **3**:38
    flamingo, greater **4**:6
    goose, Canada **4**:25
    goose, snow **4**:26
    grosbeak, evening **4**:28

grosbeak, rose-breasted **4**:29
gull, laughing **4**:31
heron, great blue **4**:35
heron, green-backed **4**:36
hornbill, great **4**:40
hornbill, rhinoceros **4**:41
hummingbird, broad-tailed
    4:43
hummingbird, ruby-throated
    4:44
ibis, scarlet **5**:8
jay, blue **5**:14
kingfisher **5**:18
kookaburra **5**:21
loon, common **5**:36
mallard **5**:40
meadowlark, eastern **6**:7
mockingbird **6**:9
nightingale **6**:30
oriole, golden **6**:36
osprey **6**:38
ostrich **6**:39
owl, barn **6**:42
owl, boreal **6**:43
owl, great horned **6**:44
owl, monk **7**:5
owl, screech **7**:6
owl, snowy **7**:7
parakeet, monk **7**:12
parrot, yellow-headed **7**:13
peafowl, Indian **7**:16
penguin, Adelie penguin **7**:18
penguin, chinstrap **7**:19
penguin, king **7**:20
penguin, little blue **7**:21
penguin, Magellanic **7**:22
pheasant, ring-necked **7**:23
pigeon, passenger **7**:25
pintail **7**:26
puffin, Atlantic **7**:29
quail, common **7**:32
raven, common **7**:37
rhea, Darwin's **7**:38
roadrunner, greater **7**:43
robin, American **7**:44
sandpiper, common **8**:10
sapsucker, yellow-bellied **8**:11
snipe, common **8**:42
sparrow, house **8**:43
starling, common **9**:12
swallow, barn **9**:15
swallow, cliff **9**:16
swan, black **9**:17
swan, trumpeter **9**:18
tern, Arctic **9**:25
tern, common **9**:26
titmouse, tufted **9**:31
toucan, toco **9**:36
turkey **9**:40
turkey, Latham's brush **9**:41
turtledove **10**:9
vulture, turkey **10**:11
warbler, Tennessee **10**:14
whippoorwill **10**:32
woodpecker, acorn **10**:37
woodpecker, ivory-billed
    10:38
woodpecker, red-headed **10**:39
wren, house **10**:40
bison, American **1**:37
black bear **1**:29
black bear, Asiatic **1**:28
blackbird, red-winged **1**:38
black carpenter ant **1**:12
black-footed ferret **3**:40
black howler monkey **6**:12
black rhinoceros **7**:39
black spider monkey **6**:13
black swan **9**:17
black widow spider **8**:44
blond tarantula, desert **9**:22
bluebird, eastern **1**:39
bluebird, mountain **1**:40
blue bird of paradise **1**:36
bluefin tuna **9**:39
bluefish **1**:41
blue heron, great **4**:35
blue jay **5**:14
blue limpet **5**:28
blue monkey **6**:14
blue shark **8**:24

blue skate **8**:35
blue whale **10**:20
boa, emerald tree **1**:43
boa constrictor **1**:42
bobcat **1**:44
bobolink **2**:5
boll weevil **10**:19
bonefish **2**:6
booby, masked **2**:7
booby, red-footed **2**:8
boreal owl **6**:43
bottle-nosed dolphin **3**:22
box turtle, common **9**:42
box turtle, ornate **10**:6
brain coral **2**:42
Brazilian tapir **9**:20
brindled gnu (wildebeest) **4**:23
broad-tailed hummingbird **4**:43
brown bear **1**:30
brown hyena **5**:5
brown lemur **5**:24
brush turkey, Latham's **9**:41
bufflehead **2**:9
bug, bed **1**:32
bullfrog **2**:10
bullfrog, African **2**:11
bumblebee, American **2**:12
Burgundy snail (edible snail)
    8:38
butterflies *see also* moths
    monarch **2**:13
    nymph, common wood **6**:31
buzzard, common **2**:14

C

caiman, dwarf **2**:15
California condor **2**:40
California moray **6**:21
California sea lion **8**:15
camel, Arabian **2**:16
camel, Bactrian **2**:17
Canada goose **4**:25
Canadian lynx **5**:37
Canadian otter **6**:40
cape pangolin **7**:11
capuchin, white-throated **2**:18
caracal **2**:19
cardinal **2**:20
Caribbean spiny lobster **5**:35
carpenter ant, black **1**:12
cat, sand **2**:21
catamount (puma) **7**:30
caterpillar, woolly bear **2**:22
cat shark, small-spotted **8**:28
centipede, house **2**:23
chacma baboon **1**:20
channeled whelk **10**:31
char, Arctic **2**:24
cheetah **2**:25
cheetah, king **2**:26
chimpanzee **2**:27
chimpanzee, pygmy **2**:28
chinchilla **2**:29
chinook salmon **8**:7
chinstrap penguin **7**:19
cicada, seventeen-year **2**:30
clam, Atlantic razor **2**:31
clam, giant **2**:32
clam, soft-shelled **2**:33
cliff swallow **9**:16
clown fish **3**:43
cobra, Asian **2**:34
cockatiel **2**:35
cockatoo, sulphur-crested **2**:36
cockroach, American **2**:37
common, for names beginning
    see next part of name
conch, queen **2**:38
condor, Andean **2**:39
condor, California **2**:40
constrictor, boa **1**:42
copperhead **2**:41
coral, brain **2**:42
coral, large flower **2**:43
cottonmouth **2**:44
cougar (puma) **7**:30
crabs
    Atlantic marsh fiddler **3**:41
    Florida stone **3**:6

crabs (cont.)
  giant hermit **3**:7
  horseshoe **3**:8
crane, common **3**:9
crane, whooping **3**:10
cricket, house **3**:11
crocodile, Nile **3**:12
crocodile, saltwater **3**:13
Cuban tree frog **4**:13

D

daddy longlegs (harvestman) **3**:14
Darwin's rhea **7**:38
De Brazza's monkey **6**:16
deer, mule **3**:15
deer, white-tailed **3**:16
desert blond tarantula **9**:22
desert iguana **5**:9
desert lynx (caracal) **2**:19
desert tortoise **9**:34
devil, Tasmanian **3**:17
dhole, Asian **3**:18
diademed guenon (blue monkey)
  6:14
diamondback rattlesnake, western
  7:36
dingo **3**:19
dogfish (small-spotted cat shark)
  8:28
dogs
  Asian dhole **3**:18
  dingo **3**:19
  raccoon dog **3**:20
dolphin, Amazon **3**:21
dolphin, bottle-nosed **3**:22
dolphin, Commerson's **3**:23
dolphin, common **3**:24
dolphin, spotted **3**:25
donkey **3**:26
dove, turtle **10**:9
dove, white-winged **3**:27
drill **3**:28
duck-billed platypus **7**:27
duck hawk (peregrine falcon)
  3:38
ducks
  bufflehead **2**:9
  mallard **5**:40
  mandarin **3**:29
  pintail **7**:26
  ruddy **3**:30
  wood **3**:31
dwarf caiman **2**:15

E

eagle, bald **3**:32
earthworm (nightcrawler) **3**:33
eastern bluebird **1**:39
eastern gray squirrel **9**:9
eastern grey kangaroo **5**:16
eastern meadowlark **6**:7
eastern oyster **7**:8
eastern ribbon snake **8**:40
eastern spotted skunk **8**:36
eastern subterranean termite **9**:24
eastern yellow jacket **10**:42
edible sea urchin **8**:17
edible snail **8**:38
eel, electric **3**:34
egret, great white (great blue
  heron) **4**:35
egret, snowy **3**:35
electric eel **3**:34
elephant, African **3**:36
elephant, Asian **3**:37
elephant seal, northern **8**:22
emerald tree boa **1**:43
emperor tamarin **9**:19
endangered animals
  ass, African wild **1**:18
  aye-aye **1**:19
  baboon, gelada **1**:21
  bear, polar **1**:31
  bobcat **1**:44
  camel, Bactrian **2**:17
  cat, sand **2**:21
  cheetah **2**:25
  cheetah, king **2**:26
  chimpanzee, pygmy **2**:28
  chinchilla **2**:29

condor, Andean **2**:39
condor, California **2**:40
crab, horseshoe **3**:8
crane, whooping **3**:10
crocodile, saltwater **3**:13
dhole, Asian **3**:18
dingo **3**:19
drill **3**:28
eagle, bald **3**:32
elephant, African **3**:36
falcon, peregrine **3**:38
ferret, black-footed **3**:40
gibbon, hoolock **4**:21
gorilla **4**:27
hyena, brown **5**:5
jaguar **5**:13
lemur, brown **5**:24
lemur, ring-tailed **5**:25
leopard **5**:26
leopard, snow **5**:27
lynx, Canadian **5**:37
macaque, liontail **5**:39
marmoset, common **6**:5
monkey, black howler **6**:12
monkey, proboscis **6**:18
ocelot **6**:32
orangutan **6**:35
oryx, Arabian **6**:37
ostrich **6**:39
otter, sea **6**:41
panda, giant **7**:9
panda, red **7**:10
pangolin, cape **7**:11
puma **7**:30
rhea, Darwin's **7**:38
rhinoceros, black **7**:39
rhinoceros, great Indian **7**:40
rhinoceros, Sumatran **7**:41
rhinoceros, white **7**:42
salmon, chinook **8**:7
tapir, Brazilian **9**:20
Tasmanian devil **3**:17
tiger, Bengal **9**:28
tiger, Siberian **9**:29
tiger, Sumatra **9**:30
tortoise, desert **9**:34
tortoise, Galápagos **9**:35
turtle, green sea **10**:5
vicuña **10**:10
vulture, turkey **10**:11
whale, blue **10**:20
whale, fin **10**:22
whale, gray **10**:23
whale, sperm **10**:30
yak **10**:41
ermine (long-tailed weasel) **10**:18
estuarine crocodile (saltwater
  crocodile) **3**:13
Eurasian badger **1**:24
evening grosbeak **4**:28
extinct animals
  pigeon, passenger **7**:25
  wolf, Tasmanian **10**:34
  woodpecker, ivory-billed
    10:38

F

fairy penguin (little blue penguin)
  7:21
falcon, peregrine **3**:38
false killer whale **10**:21
fennec **3**:39
ferret, black-footed **3**:40
fiddler, Atlantic marsh **3**:41
fighting fish, Siamese **3**:44
fin whale **10**:22
fire ant **1**:13
firefly, North American **3**:42
fish
  angelfish **1**:9
  archerfish **1**:15
  barracuda, great **1**:26
  bass, striped **1**:27
  bluefish **2**:6
  bonefish **2**:6
  char, Arctic **2**:24
  clown fish **3**:43
  eel, electric **3**:34
  gar, Florida **4**:17
  goldfish **4**:24
  guppy **4**:32

herring, Atlantic **4**:37
lamprey, sea **5**:22
manta, giant **5**:43
moray, California **6**:21
parrotfish, queen **7**:14
parrotfish, rainbow **7**:15
porcupinefish **7**:28
sailfin, giant **8**:5
salmon, Atlantic **8**:6
salmon, chinook **8**:7
salmon, sockeye **8**:8
sea horse, common **8**:14
shark, blue **8**:24
shark, great white **8**:25
shark, nurse **8**:26
shark, shortfin mako **8**:27
shark, small-spotted cat **8**:28
shark, tiger **8**:29
shark, whale **8**:30
Siamese fighting fish **3**:44
skate, blue **8**:35
snapper, red **8**:41
stingray, Atlantic **9**:13
sunfish, ocean **9**:14
tarpon **9**:23
tetra, flame **9**:27
trout, lake **9**:37
trout, rainbow **9**:38
tuna, bluefin **9**:39
zebrafish **10**:44
fisher **4**:5
flame tetra **9**:27
flamingo, greater **4**:6
Florida gar **4**:17
Florida stone crab **3**:6
flower coral, large **2**:43
fly, common fruit **4**:7
fly, tsetse **4**:8
flying squirrel, southern **9**:11
fox, Arctic **4**:9
fox, gray **4**:10
fox, kit **4**:11
fox, red **4**:12
frogs *see also* toads
  bullfrog **2**:10
  bullfrog, African **2**:11
  Cuban tree **4**:13
  green **4**:14
  peeper, spring **7**:17
  poison dart **4**:15
  wood **4**:16
fruit fly, common **4**:7
fur seal, northern **8**:23

G

Galápagos tortoise **9**:35
gar, Florida **4**:17
garden spider **9**:5
garter snake, common **8**:39
gazelle, Thomson's **4**:18
gecko, Moorish wall **4**:19
gelada baboon **1**:21
gerbil **4**:20
giant anteater **1**:14
giant clam **2**:32
giant hermit crab **3**:7
giant manta **5**:43
giant Pacific octopus **6**:34
giant panda **7**:9
giant sailfin **8**:5
giant water bug **10**:16
gibbon, hoolock **4**:21
giraffe **4**:22
gnu, brindled (wildebeest) **4**:23
golden dog (Asian dhole) **3**:18
golden jackal **5**:12
golden oriole **6**:36
goldfish **4**:24
goose, Canada **4**:25
goose, snow **4**:26
gorilla **4**:27
gray fox **4**:10
gray seal **8**:19
gray squirrel, eastern **9**:9
gray whale **10**:23
gray wolf **10**:33
great barracuda **1**:26
great blue heron **4**:35
greater flamingo **4**:6
greater roadrunner **7**:43
great hornbill **4**:40

great horned owl **6**:44
great Indian rhinoceros **7**:40
great white egret (great blue
  heron) **4**:35
great white shark **8**:25
green anaconda **1**:8
green-backed heron **4**:36
green frog **4**:14
green iguana **5**:10
green mamba **5**:41
green sea turtle **10**:5
grey, kangaroo eastern **5**:16
grizzly bear (brown bear) **1**:30
grosbeak, evening **4**:28
grosbeak, rose-breasted **4**:29
groundhog (woodchuck) **10**:36
ground squirrel, Arctic **9**:8
guenon, diademed (blue monkey)
  6:14
guinea pig **4**:30
gull, laughing **4**:31
guppy **4**:32
gypsy moth **6**:24

H

hairy armadillo, screaming **1**:16
hamadryas baboon **1**:22
hamster, common **4**:33
harbor seal **8**:20
hare, snowshoe **4**:34
harp seal **8**:21
harvestman (daddy longlegs) **3**:14
hawk, duck (peregrine falcon)
  3:38
headfish (ocean sunfish) **9**:14
hermit crab, giant **3**:7
heron, great blue **4**:35
heron, green-backed **4**:36
herring, Atlantic **4**:37
hippopotamus **4**:38
hippopotamus, pygmy **4**:39
honey bee **1**:33
hoolock gibbon **4**:21
hornbill, great **4**:40
hornbill, rhinoceros **4**:41
horned owl, great **6**:44
horsefly, American **4**:42
horseshoe crab **3**:8
house centipede **2**:23
house cricket **3**:11
house mouse **6**:26
house sparrow **8**:43
house spider **9**:6
house wren **10**:40
howler monkey, black **6**:12
hummingbird, broad-tailed **4**:43
hummingbird, ruby-throated **4**:44
humpback whale **10**:24
hyena, brown **5**:5
hyena, laughing **5**:6

I

ibex, alpine **5**:7
ibis, scarlet **5**:8
iguana, desert **5**:9
iguana, green **5**:10
impala **5**:11
Indian peafowl **7**:16
Indian rhinoceros, great **7**:40
Indo-Pacific crocodile (saltwater
  crocodile) **3**:13
invertebrates, other
  clam, Atlantic razor **2**:31
  clam, giant **2**:32
  clam, soft-shelled **2**:33
  conch, queen **2**:38
  coral, brain **2**:42
  coral, large flower **2**:43
  earthworm (nightcrawler) **3**:33
  jellyfish, moon **5**:15
  leech, medicinal **5**:23
  limpet, blue **5**:28
  man-of-war, Portuguese **5**:42
  mussel, zebra **6**:29
  octopus, common **6**:33
  octopus, giant Pacific **6**:34
  oyster, eastern **7**:8
  sand dollar, common **8**:9
  scallop, bay **8**:12
  sea fan **8**:13

sea star, common **8**:16
sea urchin, edible **8**:17
snail, edible **8**:38
whelk, channeled **10**:31
Isabella tiger moth (woolly bear caterpillar) **2**:22
ivory-billed woodpecker **10**:38

J-K

jackal, golden **5**:12
jaguar **5**:13
Japanese beetle **1**:34
jay, blue **5**:14
jellyfish, moon **5**:15
jungle dog (Asian dhole) **3**:18
kangaroo, eastern grey **5**:16
kangaroo, red **5**:17
killer whale **10**:25
killer whale, false **10**:21
king cheetah **2**:26
kingfisher **5**:18
king penguin **7**:20
king salmon (chinook salmon) **8**:7
kingsnake, common **5**:19
kit fox **4**:11
koala **5**:20
Kodiak bear (brown bear) **1**:30
kookaburra **5**:21

L

lake trout **9**:37
lamprey, sea **5**:22
large flower coral **2**:43
Latham's brush turkey **9**:41
laughing gull **4**:31
laughing hyena **5**:6
leech, medicinal **5**:23
lemur, brown **5**:24
lemur, ring-tailed **5**:25
leopard **5**:26
leopard, snow **5**:27
lightning bugs (fireflies) **3**:42
limpet, blue **5**:28
linsang, banded **5**:29
lion **5**:30
liontail macaque **5**:39
little blue penguin (fairy penguin) **7**:21
lizard, armadillo **5**:31
lizard, ornate tree **5**:32
llama **5**:33
lobster, American **5**:34
lobster, Caribbean spiny **5**:35
long-eared (screech owl) **7**:6
long-finned pilot whale **10**:26
long-tailed weasel **10**:18
loon, common **5**:36
luna moth **6**:25
lynx, Canadian **5**:37
lynx, desert (caracal) **2**:19

M

macaque, Barbary **5**:38
Magellanic penguin **7**:22
mako shark, shortfin **8**:27
mallard **5**:40
mamba, green **5**:41
mammals
  aardvark **1**:5
  anteater, giant **1**:14
  armadillo, screaming hairy **1**:16
  ass, African wild **1**:18
  aye-aye **1**:19
  baboon, chacma **1**:20
  baboon, gelada **1**:21
  baboon, hamadryas **1**:22
  baboon, yellow **1**:23
  badger, Eurasian **1**:24
  bandicoot, spiny **1**:25
  bear, Asiatic black **1**:28
  bear, black **1**:29
  bear, brown **1**:30
  bear, polar **1**:31
  beluga **1**:35
  bison, American **1**:37
  bobcat **1**:44
  camel, Arabian **2**:16
  camel, Bactrian **2**:17

capuchin, white-throated **2**:18
caracal **2**:19
cat, sand **2**:21
cheetah **2**:25
cheetah, king **2**:26
chimpanzee **2**:27
chimpanzee, pygmy **2**:28
chinchilla **2**:29
coyote **3**:5
deer, mule **3**:15
deer, white-tailed **3**:16
dhole, Asian **3**:18
dingo **3**:19
dog, raccoon **3**:20
dolphin, Amazon **3**:21
dolphin, bottle-nosed **3**:22
dolphin, Commerson's **3**:23
dolphin, common **3**:24
dolphin, spotted **3**:25
donkey **3**:26
drill **3**:28
elephant, African **3**:36
elephant, Asian **3**:37
fennec **3**:39
ferret, black-footed **3**:40
fisher **4**:5
fox, Arctic **4**:9
fox, gray **4**:10
fox, kit **4**:11
fox, red **4**:12
gazelle, Thomson's **4**:18
gerbil **4**:20
gibbon, hoolock **4**:21
giraffe **4**:22
gnu, brindled (wildebeest) **4**:23
gorilla **4**:27
guinea pig **4**:30
hamster, common **4**:33
hare, snowshoe **4**:34
hippopotamus **4**:38
hippopotamus, pygmy **4**:39
hyena, brown **5**:5
hyena, laughing **5**:6
ibex, alpine **5**:7
impala **5**:11
jackal, golden **5**:12
jaguar **5**:13
kangaroo, eastern grey **5**:16
kangaroo, red **5**:17
koala **5**:20
lemur, brown **5**:24
lemur, ring-tailed **5**:25
leopard **5**:26
leopard, snow **5**:27
linsang, banded **5**:29
lion **5**:30
llama **5**:33
lynx, Canadian **5**:37
macaque, Barbary **5**:38
macaque, liontail **5**:39
marmoset, common **6**:5
marten, American **6**:6
mink, American **6**:8
mole, star-nosed **6**:10
mongoose, banded **6**:11
monkey, black howler **6**:12
monkey, black spider **6**:13
monkey, blue **6**:14
monkey, common squirrel **6**:15
monkey, De Brazza's **6**:16
monkey, night **6**:17
monkey, proboscis **6**:18
monkey, rhesus **6**:19
moose **6**:20
mouse, house **6**:26
muskox **6**:27
muskrat **6**:28
ocelot **6**:32
orangutan **6**:35
oryx, Arabian **6**:37
otter, Canadian **6**:40
otter, sea **6**:41
panda, giant **7**:9
panda, red **7**:10
pangolin, cape **7**:11
pig, bearded **7**:24
platypus, duck-billed **7**:27
puma **7**:30
raccoon **7**:33

rhinoceros, black **7**:39
rhinoceros, great Indian **7**:40
rhinoceros, Sumatran **7**:41
rhinoceros, white **7**:42
seal, bearded **8**:18
seal, gray **8**:19
seal, harbor **8**:20
seal, harp **8**:21
seal, northern elephant **8**:22
seal, northern fur **8**:23
sea lion, California **8**:15
sheep, bighorn **8**:31
skunk, eastern spotted **8**:36
squirrel, Arctic ground **9**:8
squirrel, eastern gray **9**:9
squirrel, red **9**:10
squirrel, southern flying **9**:11
tamarin, emperor **9**:19
tapir, Brazilian **9**:20
Tasmanian devil **3**:17
tiger, Bengal **9**:28
tiger, Siberian **9**:29
tiger, Sumatra **9**:30
vicuña **10**:10
walrus, Atlantic **10**:12
walrus, Pacific **10**:13
warthog **10**:15
weasel, long-tailed **10**:18
whale, blue **10**:20
whale, false killer **10**:21
whale, fin **10**:22
whale, gray **10**:23
whale, humpback **10**:24
whale, killer **10**:25
whale, long-finned pilot **10**:26
whale, Pacific pilot **10**:27
whale, pygmy right **10**:28
whale, pygmy sperm **10**:29
whale, sperm **10**:30
wolf, gray **10**:33
wolf, Tasmanian **10**:34
wombat, common **10**:35
woodchuck **10**:36
yak **10**:41
zebra, plains **10**:43
mandarin duck **3**:29
man-of-war, Portuguese **5**:42
manta, giant **5**:43
mantis, praying **5**:44
marmoset, common **6**:5
marsupials
  bandicoot, spiny **1**:25
  common wombat **10**:35
  eastern grey kangaroo **5**:16
  koala **5**:20
  red kangaroo **5**:17
  Tasmanian devil **3**:17
  Tasmanian wolf **10**:34
marten, American **6**:6
masked booby **2**:7
meadowlark, eastern **6**:7
medicinal leech **5**:23
mink, American **6**:8
mockingbird **6**:9
mola (ocean sunfish) **9**:14
mole, star-nosed **6**:10
monarch butterfly **2**:13
mongoose, banded **6**:11
monkeys *see also* baboons
  black howler **6**:12
  black spider **6**:13
  blue **6**:14
  capuchin, white-throated **2**:18
  common squirrel **6**:15
  De Brazza's **6**:16
  macaque, Barbary **5**:38
  macaque, liontail **5**:39
  marmoset, common **6**:5
  night **6**:17
  proboscis **6**:18
  rhesus **6**:19
monk parakeet **7**:12
moon bear (Asiatic black bear) **1**:28
moonfish (ocean sunfish) **9**:14
moon jellyfish **5**:15
Moorish wall gecko **4**:19
moose **6**:20
moray, California **6**:21
mosquito **6**:22

moths *see also* butterflies
  Atlas **6**:23
  gypsy **6**:24
  Isabella tiger (woolly bear) **2**:22
  luna **6**:25
mountain bluebird **1**:40
mountain lion (puma) **7**:30
mouse, house **6**:26
mud turtle, common **9**:43
mule deer **3**:15
muskox **6**:27
muskrat **6**:28
musk turtle, common **9**:44
mussel, zebra **6**:29

N

nightcrawler (earthworm) **3**:33
nightingale **6**:30
night monkey **6**:17
Nile crocodile **3**:12
North American firefly **3**:42
northern elephant seal **8**:22
northern fur seal **8**:23
northern pink shrimp **8**:33
nurse shark **8**:26
nymph, common wood **6**:31

O

ocean sunfish **9**:14
ocelot **6**:32
octopus, common **6**:33
octopus, giant Pacific **6**:34
orangutan **6**:35
oriole, golden **6**:36
ornate box turtle **10**:6
ornate tree lizard **5**:32
oryx, Arabian **6**:37
osprey **6**:38
ostrich **6**:39
otter, Canadian **6**:40
otter, sea **6**:41
owl, barn **6**:42
owl, boreal **6**:43
owl, great horned **6**:44
owl, pygmy **7**:5
owl, screech **7**:6
owl, snowy **7**:7
oyster, eastern **7**:8

P

Pacific octopus, giant **6**:34
Pacific pilot whale **10**:27
Pacific walrus **10**:13
painted turtle **10**:7
panda, giant **7**:9
panda, red **7**:10
pangolin, cape **7**:11
panther (puma) **7**:30
parakeet, monk **7**:12
parrot, yellow-headed **7**:13
parrotfish, queen **7**:14
parrotfish, rainbow **7**:15
passenger pigeon **7**:25
peafowl, Indian **7**:16
peeper, spring **7**:17
penguin, Adelie penguin **7**:18
penguin, chinstrap **7**:19
penguin, king **7**:20
penguin, little blue **7**:21
penguin, Magellanic **7**:22
peregrine falcon **3**:38
pheasant, ring-necked **7**:23
pig, bearded **7**:24
pigeon, passenger **7**:25
pilot whale, long-finned **10**:26
pilot whale, Pacific **10**:27
pink shrimp, northern **8**:33
pintail **7**:26
plains zebra **10**:43
platypus, duck-billed **7**:27
poison dart frog **4**:15
polar bear **1**:31
porcupinefish **7**:28
Portuguese man-of war **5**:42
prairie rattlesnake **7**:34
praying mantis **5**:44
proboscis monkey **6**:18
puffin, Atlantic **7**:29
puma **7**:30

pygmy chimpanzee **2**:28
pygmy hippopotamus **4**:39
pygmy owl **7**:5
pygmy right whale **10**:28
pygmy sperm whale **10**:29
python, ball **7**:31

Q-R

quail, common **7**:32
queen conch **2**:38
queen parrotfish **7**:14
raccoon **7**:33
raccoon dog **3**:20
rainbow parrotfish **7**:15
rainbow trout **9**:38
rattlesnake, prairie **7**:34
rattlesnake, timber **7**:35
rattlesnake, western diamondback **7**:36
raven, common **7**:37
razor clam, Atlantic **2**:31
red-breasted baboon (gelada baboon) **1**:21
red dog (Asian dhole) **3**:18
red-footed booby **2**:8
red fox **4**:12
red-headed woodpecker **10**:39
red hermit crab (giant hermit crab) **3**:7
red kangaroo **5**:17
red panda **7**:10
red snapper **8**:41
red squirrel **9**:10
red-winged blackbird **1**:38
reptiles *see also* snakes
    alligator, American **1**:7
    caiman, dwarf **2**:15
    crocodile, Nile **3**:12
    crocodile, saltwater **3**:13
    gecko, Moorish wall **4**:19
    iguana, desert **5**:9
    iguana, green **5**:10
    lizard, armadillo **5**:31
    lizard, ornate tree **5**:32
    slider **8**:37
    tortoise, desert **9**:34
    tortoise, Galápagos **9**:35
    turtle, common box **9**:42
    turtle, common mud **9**:43
    turtle, common musk **9**:44
    turtle, green sea **10**:5
    turtle, ornate box **10**:6
    turtle, painted **10**:7
    turtle, snapping **10**:8
rhea, Darwin's **7**:38
rhesus monkey **6**:19
rhinoceros, black **7**:39
rhinoceros, great Indian **7**:40
rhinoceros, Sumatran **7**:41
rhinoceros, white **7**:42
rhinoceros hornbill **4**:41
ribbon snake, eastern **8**:40
right whale, pygmy **10**:28
ring-necked pheasant **7**:23
ring-tailed lemur **5**:25
roadrunner, greater **7**:43
robin, American **7**:44
rose-breasted grosbeak **4**:29
ruby-throated hummingbird **4**:44
ruddy duck **3**:30

S

sailfin, giant **8**:5
salmon, Atlantic **8**:6
salmon, chinook **8**:7
salmon, sockeye **8**:8
saltwater crocodile **3**:13
sand cat **2**:21
sand dollar, common **8**:9
sandpiper, common **8**:10
sapsucker, yellow-bellied **8**:11

scallop, bay **8**:12
scarlet ibis **5**:8
screaming hairy armadillo **1**:16
screech owl **7**:6
sea cake (common sand dollar) **8**:9
sea fan **8**:13
sea horse, common **8**:14
seal, bearded **8**:18
seal, gray **8**:19
seal, harbor **8**:20
seal, harp **8**:21
seal, northern elephant **8**:22
seal, northern fur **8**:23
sea lamprey **5**:22
sea lion, California **8**:15
sea otter **6**:41
sea star, common **8**:16
sea turtle, green **10**:5
sea urchin, edible **8**:17
seventeen-year cicada **2**:30
shark, blue **8**:24
shark, great white **8**:25
shark, nurse **8**:26
shark, shortfin mako **8**:27
shark, small-spotted cat **8**:28
shark, tiger **8**:29
shark, whale **8**:30
sheep, bighorn **8**:31
shivering owl (screech owl) **7**:6
shortfin mako shark **8**:27
shrimp, common **8**:32
shrimp, northern pink **8**:33
Siamese fighting fish **3**:44
Siberian tiger **9**:29
Siberian wild dog (Asian dhole) **3**:18
sidewinder **8**:34
skate, blue **8**:35
skunk, eastern spotted **8**:36
slender-beaked dolphin (spotted dolphin) **3**:25
slider **8**:37
small-spotted cat shark **8**:28
snail, edible **8**:38
snakebird (American anhinga) **1**:10
snakes
    anaconda, green **1**:8
    asp **1**:17
    boa, emerald tree **1**:43
    boa constrictor **1**:42
    cobra, Asian **2**:34
    copperhead **2**:41
    cottonmouth **2**:44
    garter snake, common **8**:39
    kingsnake, common **5**:19
    mamba, green **5**:41
    python, ball **7**:31
    rattlesnake, prairie **7**:34
    rattlesnake, timber **7**:35
    rattlesnake, western diamondback **7**:36
    ribbon snake, eastern **8**:40
    sidewinder **8**:34
snapper, red **8**:41
snapping turtle **10**:8
snipe, common **8**:42
snow goose **4**:26
snow leopard **5**:27
snowshoe hare **4**:34
snowy egret **3**:35
snowy owl **7**:7
sockeye salmon **8**:8
soft-shelled clam **2**:33
southern flying squirrel **9**:11
spadefoot toad, western **9**:33
sparrow, house **8**:43
sperm whale **10**:30
sperm whale, pygmy **10**:29
spider monkey, black **6**:13

spiders
    black widow **8**:44
    garden **9**:5
    house **9**:6
    tarantula **9**:21
    tarantula, desert blond **9**:22
    wolf **9**:7
spiny bandicoot **1**:25
spiny lobster, Caribbean **5**:35
spotted dolphin **3**:25
spotted skunk, eastern **8**:36
spring peeper **7**:17
square-lipped rhinoceros (white rhinoceros) **7**:42
squirrel, Arctic ground **9**:8
squirrel, eastern gray **9**:9
squirrel, red **9**:10
squirrel, southern flying **9**:11
squirrel monkey, common **6**:15
starfish (sea star) **8**:16
starling, common **9**:12
star-nosed mole **6**:10
steelhead trout (rainbow trout) **9**:38
stingray, Atlantic **9**:13
stone crab, Florida **3**:6
striped bass **1**:27
subterranean termite, eastern **9**:24
sulphur-crested cockatoo **2**:36
Sumatran rhinoceros **7**:41
Sumatra tiger **9**:30
sunfish, ocean **9**:14
swallow, barn **9**:15
swallow, cliff **9**:16
swan, black **9**:17
swan, trumpeter **9**:18

T

tamarin, emperor **9**:19
tapir, Brazilian **9**:20
tarantula **9**:21
tarantula, desert blond **9**:22
tarpon **9**:23
Tasmanian devil **3**:17
Tasmanian wolf **10**:34
Tengmalm's owl (boreal owl) **6**:43
Tennessee warbler **10**:14
termite, eastern subterranean **9**:24
tern, Arctic **9**:25
tern, common **9**:26
tetra, flame **9**:27
Thomson's gazelle **4**:18
tiger, Bengal **9**:28
tiger, Siberian **9**:29
tiger, Sumatra **9**:30
tiger moth, Isabella (woolly bear caterpillar) **2**:22
tiger shark **8**:29
timber rattlesnake **7**:35
titmouse, tufted **9**:31
toads *see also* frogs
    American **9**:32
    western spadefoot **9**:33
toco toucan **9**:36
tortoises *see also* turtles
    desert **9**:34
    Galñpagos **9**:35
toucan, toco **9**:36
tree boa, emerald **1**:43
tree fox (gray fox) **4**:10
tree frog, Cuban **4**:13
tree lizard, ornate **5**:32
trout, lake **9**:37
trout, rainbow **9**:38
trumpeter swan **9**:18
tsetse fly **4**:8
tufted titmouse **9**:31
tuna, bluefin **9**:39
turkey **9**:40
turkey, Latham's brush **9**:41

turkey vulture **10**:11
turtledove **10**:9
turtles *see also* tortoises
    common box **9**:42
    common mud **9**:43
    common musk **9**:44
    green sea **10**:5
    ornate box **10**:6
    painted **10**:7
    slider **8**:37
    snapping **10**:8

U-V-W

vicuña **10**:10
vulture, turkey **10**:11
wall gecko, Moorish **4**:19
walrus, Atlantic **10**:12
walrus, Pacific **10**:13
wandering albatross **1**:6
warbler, Tennessee **10**:14
warthog **10**:15
water bug, giant **10**:16
water bug (American cockroach) **2**:37
water dog, Alabama **10**:17
weasel, long-tailed **10**:18
weevil, boll **10**:19
western diamondback rattlesnake **7**:36
western spadefoot toad **9**:33
whales
    beluga **1**:35
    blue **10**:20
    false killer **10**:21
    fin **10**:22
    gray **10**:23
    humpback **10**:24
    killer **10**:25
    long-finned pilot **10**:26
    Pacific pilot **10**:27
    pygmy right **10**:28
    pygmy sperm **10**:29
    sperm **10**:30
whale shark **8**:30
whelk, channeled **10**:31
whippoorwill **10**:32
white egret, great (great blue heron) **4**:35
white oryx (Arabian oryx) **6**:37
white rhinoceros **7**:42
white shark, great **8**:25
white-tailed deer **3**:16
white-throated capuchin **2**:18
white whale (beluga) **1**:35
white-winged dove **3**:27
whooping crane **3**:10
wild ass, African **1**:18
wildebeest (brindled gnu) **4**:23
wolf, gray **10**:33
wolf, Tasmanian **10**:34
wolf spider **9**:7
wombat, common **10**:35
woodchuck **10**:36
wood duck **3**:31
wood frog **4**:16
wood nymph, common **6**:31
woodpecker, acorn **10**:37
woodpecker, ivory-billed **10**:38
woodpecker, red-headed **10**:39
woolly bear caterpillar **2**:22
wren, house **10**:40

X-Y-Z

yak **10**:41
yellow baboon **1**:23
yellow-bellied sapsucker **8**:11
yellow-headed parrot **7**:13
yellow jacket, eastern **10**:42
zebra, plains **10**:43
zebrafish **10**:44
zebra mussel **6**:29